population to that of working age. While elderly people have been increasing as a proportion of the working population in the United Kingdom, the ratio of children (the other major dependency group) to working population has fallen (Table 1.2). At the same time the population of working age has grown, thus little change is expected in dependency ratios 'until the rapid increase in the number of elderly, when members of the post-World War II birth cohorts start to retire' (Craig, 1983).

Table 1.1 Elderly people in private households by sex, age and type of household. Great Britain 1986 (percentages)

Household type	Males						Females					
	All 65+	65-69	70-74	75-79	80-84	85+	All 65+	65-69	70-74	75-79	80-84	85+
With spouse												
and others	11	16	9	6	7	7	5	7	5	2	2	4
no others	62	65	65	65	50	38	33	50	39	28	13	8
Total with spouse	**73**	**81**	**74**	**71**	**57**	**45**	**38**	**57**	**44**	**30**	**15**	**12**
Without spouse but with:												
children/children-in-law	3	2	2	5	4	15	9	5	6	8	16	23
siblings	2	2	1	2	2	3	3	3	3	5	4	2
others	2	2	1	1	3	0	2	2	2	2	2	2
Total without spouse/ with others	**7**	**4**	**4**	**8**	**9**	**18**	**14**	**10**	**11**	**15**	**22**	**27**
Living alone	20	13	21	21	34	37	48	33	45	55	62	61

Source: General Household Survey 1986, table 12.2.

However there are caveats to be made about the use and interpretation of dependency ratios. For example, it is the population of working age, not that proportion of the population which is actually in employment, that is used to calculate the ratios; changes in the rate of unemployment may thus compromise their usefulness.

Table 1.2 Dependent population as a percentage of population of working age

Dependent population	Census-based estimates		Mid-1981 based projections			
	1971	1981	1991	2001	2011	2021
Children under 16	12.2	10.9	10.3	11.4	10.8	11.0
Pensionable age*	8.0	9.0	9.4	9.2	9.8	10.8
Total	**20.3**	**19.9**	**19.7**	**20.6**	**20.6**	**21.7**

**Men 65 or over and women 60 or over*

Source: Craig, 1983

Secondly, as Rimmer and Wicks (1983) have pointed out, dependency ratios are 'based on the school leaving age and on retirement age, both of which are flexible and neither of which are necessarily the point of entry to or exit from the labour force' (p. 25). Moreover, Craig (1983) has suggested that 'some kind of weighting system [in calculating dependency ratios] may be desirable', if projections about the elderly population are required, because of the greater demand on resources that is made as age increases. However, he introduces a note of caution about 'predicting' future demands: 'it must be remembered that all projections are subject to an element of uncertainty; changes in mortality patterns alone could easily make a difference of half a million people to the elderly population in 30 or 40 years' time. Comparisons about dependency ratios which involve assumptions about future births are even more tentative'.

Disability and Handicap

Not all old people, nor indeed all 'old old' people, are necessarily in need of special care. The image of the robust, active woman in her eighties acting as the lynch-pin in a family support network is one not without foundation in reality. However, it is true that the incidence and severity of disability increase with age and that older women are more likely to be disabled, and more severely so, than older men, even when differential survival is taken into account (see Table 1.3). Thus a growing population of elderly people, and one which

contains a higher proportion of women, by definition implies a growing population of people with special needs.

Recent publication of findings from the national surveys of disability, carried out in 1985, 1986 and 1988 by the Office of Population Censuses and Surveys (OPCS), has provided a very comprehensive picture of the incidence and nature of disability in Great Britain. It has been estimated that there are around 5.78 million disabled adults (16+), 0.42 million of whom live in 'communal establishments' (residential homes, hospitals and the like) and 1.2 million of whom fall into the least severe category of disability (Martin, Elliot and Meltzer, 1988). In addition there are an estimated 0.36 million children with disabilities, 5,000 of whom live in communal establishments and 33,000 of whom fall into the least severe category (Bone and Meltzer, 1989).

Table 1.3 Age distribution by severity category for men and women: adults living in private households

	Severity category*					
Men	**1-2**	**3-4**	**5-6**	**7-8**	**9-10**	**Total**
	%	%	%	%	%	%
16-59	35	37	40	36	27	36
60-74	46	40	34	34	37	41
75+	19	23	25	30	36	23
Base:	1715	1019	702	476	231	4142
Women						
16-59	31	32	30	26	23	29
60-74	39	34	30	26	24	33
75+	31	34	40	48	53	38
Base:	1748	1433	1354	882	439	5856

**1 is the least and 10 the most serious category of disability.*

Reproduced from Martin, Meltzer and Elliot, 1988 Table 4.2

Of course, not all people who are disabled need help from day to day. Further, not all people with the same apparent degree of disability will need the same level of help. For example, the availability of aids or specially adapted housing may reduce the extent to which some people have to depend on others to help them.

The OPCS surveys showed that 22 per cent of all disabled adults living in private households required help with some form of self-care task, such as getting in and out of bed or washing, while 58 per cent needed help with household activities. In all, 60 per cent required help with one or both types of activity (Martin, White and Meltzer, 1989). Grossed up to the estimated population of disabled adults in private households, these figures suggest that there are around 1.2 million people who need help with self-care tasks, 3.1 million who need help with household tasks and 3.2 million who require help with one or both types of task.

Interestingly, the proportion of people reporting that they needed help with self-care tasks (22 per cent) was lower than the proportion reporting that they had personal care disabilities (37 per cent), despite the fact that these two elements of the survey covered the same areas of personal care — getting in and out of bed, getting in and out of a chair, washing, dressing, feeding, and getting to and using the toilet. Why there should be this discrepancy is not immediately obvious. One possibility is that the use of aids and adaptations may have reduced the need for help. Further analysis of the OPCS data may throw light on this issue.

At the time of writing, figures on the proportion of disabled children in private households who require help in their every-day activities are not available. However, it is possible to give some lower and upper estimates of the likely figures by reference to the available data.

Most disabled children below, say, ten years of age will need help from someone else by virtue of their age rather than, necessarily, their disability. Above this age those with a severity level above four (which the adult survey suggests is where the need for help from others starts to show) can be presumed to need help. Taken

together this would give the upper estimate. The lower estimate can be taken as all those children who have a personal care disability.

These calculations, again grossed up to the estimated number of children with disabilities, add between 83,000 and 320,000 to the total numbers of those requiring help in their everyday lives.

In sum, it seems that there may be anything between 3.3 million and 3.5 million individuals in Great Britain needing help from others to go about their daily activities. Even using the lower limit these surveys appear to have revealed levels of need for help in excess of previous projections. For example, Harris (1971) estimated on the basis of her survey in the late 1960s that by 1981 there would be around 1.3 million people aged 16 years or more who were appreciably, severely, or very severely incapacitated. Townsend (1979) suggested that a figure of 1.9 million people aged ten years or more was a more realistic figure, while the Equal Opportunities Commission (EOC) stated as a best estimate that 'the total number of handicapped people who are at present living at home and needing care exceeds 1.5 million' (EOC, 1982a, p. 8). In fact, as the figures presented here suggest, this figure could be over 3 million.

The Population of Carers

When the first edition of this book was produced (Parker, 1985) information on the likely numbers of informal carers had to be extrapolated from a variety of sources. This, admittedly imperfect, process led to the suggestion that, at a most conservative estimate, there were around 1.3 million people acting as principal carers to adults and children with disabilities severe enough to warrant support in their daily living.

Since then, in the same way as the OPCS surveys have thrown light on the numbers of people with disabilities in Great Britain, so the 1985 General Household Survey (Green, 1988) has indicated, for the first time, the likely numbers of informal carers in the population.

The 1985 GHS revealed that 14 per cent of people aged

16 and over 'were looking after, or providing some regular service for, someone who was sick, elderly or handicapped' (Green, 1988, p. 6). Applied to the population of Great Britain as a whole these figures suggest a total of around 6 million carers.

Obviously this is a far higher number than that suggested by the OPCS surveys of disability. However, not all of those who identified themselves as carers in the GHS were principal carers, were living in the same household as the person being cared for, or were providing care for 20 hours or more a week (see Table 1.4). When applied to the population of Great Britain, the survey report indicates 'that about 1.7 million adults are caring for someone living with them, 1.4 million are spending at least twenty hours per week or providing help or supervision and about 3.7 million are bearing the main responsibility for the care of someone' (p. 7). This last figure comes somewhere near the upper estimate, given earlier, of the number of people living in the community who require some form of help.

Table 1.4 Percentage of adults who were carers and percentages in some sub-groups of carers, by sex (Great Britain, 1985)

Percentage of people aged 16 and over who were:	Men %	Women %	All adults %
Carers	12	15	14
Caring for someone in same household*	4	4	4
Caring for someone in another private household only	8	11	10
Main carers	6	10	8
Caring for at least 20 hours per week	3	4	3

** Includes those caring for someone in same household* ***and*** *someone in another household.*

Source: Green, 1988, Table 2.1

The OPCS survey did actually ask adults living in private households whether anyone helped them with self-care or household activities. This process revealed 56 per cent of disabled adults who said that they had 'informal helpers' ie an 'unpaid relative or friend who helped this disabled adult with any of the fifteen activities [of self-care or household activities]' (Martin, White and Meltzer, 1989, p. 98). Because some people had more than one helper a total of 6,839 helpers were identified among the 10,000 people surveyed.

The report goes on further to distinguish 'informal carers', ie 'unpaid relative[s] or friend[s] who helped with any of the self-care activities', and 'main carers', the informal carers 'who, according to the disabled adult, spent the most time helping or looking after them' (ibid.). There were 1,887 main carers out of a total of 2,139 informal carers.

Applied to the total estimated population of adults with disabilities these figures suggest a total of 3.7 million informal helpers, of whom 1.2 million are carers, 1.0 million being main carers. If we assume one main carer for each disabled child living in private households (estimated by Bone and Meltzer (1989) as 354,500) the final population of main carers becomes 1.3 million. Again, these are somewhat smaller numbers than those suggested by the GHS and, indeed, by the numbers of people saying that they needed help.

This lack of exact comparability is not, of course, surprising. First, as the EOC (1982a) has pointed out, 'There is no strict equivalence between the number of handicapped people living in the community who require care and the numbers who actually receive it' (p. 9). Some dependent people live alone without informal support, others live alone with a considerable input of care from people living elsewhere. Some dependent people have only one informal carer while others may have several. Conversely, one informal carer may be responsible for more than one dependent person.

Secondly, the question used to allow carers to identify themselves in the GHS was worded to be as all-inclusive in its scope as was possible. This would, thereby, have defined as carers those who were helping people who would not necessarily have been considered as 'disabled' by the criteria used in the OPCS surveys.

Thirdly, the OPCS survey of adults asked only about help given with self-care and household activities. It probably, thereby, excluded a lot of carers of people who are mentally ill, where the main burdens of caring are not the physical tasks identified as the main part of caring for other groups (Perring, 1989).

To summarise, there are around 6 million people in Great Britain who consider themselves to be providing care for a sick, handicapped, or elderly person although rather fewer (around 3.7 million) are helping *adults* disabled enough to have been included in the OPCS surveys. In total there may be 1.3 million 'main' carers of disabled adults and children, an identical figure to that hypothesised in 1985.

Changes in the Population of Carers

Demographic and social changes have implications for the population of carers as well as the population of those to be cared for. Clearly, in the absence of longitudinal information relating specifically to carers, it is difficult to monitor such changes. However, on a number of grounds, it seems likely that the population of people available to take on informal care responsibilities has been affected in recent years.

Changes in marriage patterns

One significant change which may affect the potential pool of carers is the increase in divorce and remarriage. In 1961 the number of people divorcing per thousand married couples was 2.1; in 1986 it had risen to 13.4 (Table 1.5), although it has recently fallen back a little. Over a similar period remarriage for one or both partners, as a percentage of all marriages, had risen from 15 per cent to 34 per cent (*Social Trends* 1983, Table 2.12 and 2.15). Within this trend the proportion of marriages where one or both partners had been married previously more than doubled. One result of this re-assortment of marriage partners may be a blurring or confusing of the lines of 'responsibility' for the care of, especially, parents, step-parents and parents-in-law.

Table 1.5 Divorce and remarriage in the United Kingdom 1961-1987

	1961	1971	1976	1981	1984	1985	1986	1987
Persons divorcing per thousand married people	2.1	6.0	10.1	11.9	12.0	13.4	12.9	12.6
Estimated nos. of people who had not remarried (thousands)								
Men	101	200	405	653	846	916	988	—
Women	184	317	564	890	1104	1177	1257	—
Total	285	517	969	1543	1950	2094	2245	

Source: Social Trends 19, 1989, Table 2.12

Wicks (1982) has pointed out that the impact of divorce on carers' capacity to care is not clear. 'On the one hand, perhaps, a divorced person might welcome the social contact that caring involves. But, on the other, many may feel a necessity to seek employment (and thus have less time for caring) or may have to move to less suitable housing or may find their remarriage prospects affected by any substantial responsibility to a dependent relative' (p. 108). The impact of divorce on capacity to care is further clouded by the fact that remarriage is differential — women are less likely to remarry than men (Table 1.5) although this difference seems to be narrowing with time. This differential impact is important, not least because the financial constraints on divorced women are greater because of their lower earnings. It is only by reconstitution of families that the children of divorced women ever regain their former standard of living (Maclean and Eekelaar, 1983), and other dependent relatives of divorced women may also be affected. For example, a single parent with children and a job is unlikely to have the time to care for other dependent relatives, while a single parent with children but without a job may be unable to sustain the extra expenditure that caring for a dependent relative entails (see Chapter Three).

However, although the proportion of lone parent households has increased as a proportion of all households, they still do not constitute a large section of the population. In 1961 there were 367,000 lone parent households in Great Britain with at least one dependent child (2 per cent of all households) and in 1971 there were 515,000 (3 per cent). In 1987 lone parent households with dependent children accounted for only 5 per cent of all households. The increase in the number of single parent families *per se* thus seems likely to have a smaller impact on the population of potential carers, compared with the remarriage of divorced people (*Social Trends* 1989 Table 2.9).

Decline in the proportion of single women in the population

The 'traditional' image of the carer for elderly people is that of an unmarried daughter living in the parental home. However, over the past 100 years the proportion of single people of both sexes has fallen in Great Britain (Haskey, 1987 and Halsey, 1972, Tables 2.14 and 2.15), although the trend has been more marked for women. In 1985 only 4 per cent of women and 7 per cent of men aged 50 had never been married (Haskey, 1987). Thus the supply of single daughters (or even sons) who might take on sole responsibility for ageing parents is more limited than in the past.

Changing family size

As well as there being fewer single daughters to take on care commitments, there are now fewer children altogether. Family size has dropped steadily since the turn of the century while the proportion of childless marriages has continued to grow. The implications of these changes may be considerable: more elderly couples will have no immediate kin who might care for them as they become frail and more elderly widows and widowers will have to live by themselves after the death of their spouse; there will be fewer adult children to share the care of elderly parents (although as will be shown in Chapter 2 such care is not often fully shared even now); family networks, which might have supported primary carers, will contract or even disappear. For example, the only child of parents who are both only children themselves will not only have no siblings, but also will have no aunts, uncles or cousins. If he or she then married another only child they would have no nieces or nephews.

Women's labour market participation

Had married women remained as Beveridge characterised them — at home, bringing up their families and relying on their husbands financially — they might have been readily available to make up any short-fall in the population of carers. However, women's participation in the labour market has increased substantially over the past 20 years, almost all of this increase being accounted for by married women. In 1961 married women made up an estimated 16 per cent of the total labour force and it was expected that by 1986 they would constitute 25 per cent of the total (*Social Trends* 1983, Table 4.2).

Over the same period the proportion of unmarried women in the labour force fell slightly from 16 per cent to 14 per cent.

The increase in married women's participation appears to have been spread differentially between age groups. In 1961, 41 per cent of married women aged 20-24 years were in the labour force; by 1981 this had risen to 58 per cent. Among married women aged 25-44 years participation rose over the same period from 33 per cent to 58 per cent. The largest increase, however, took place among married women aged 45-59. Their participation rose from 33 per cent in 1961 to 62 per cent in 1981 (*Social Trends* 1983 Table 4.3). Thus, while in 1961 over 60 per cent of the population of married women aged 45-59 would, in theory, have been available to take on caring roles, by 1981 under 40 per cent were so available. This is particularly important because it is this group of women who may be most likely to have ageing parents and husbands whose health is beginning to deteriorate.

Despite increased unemployment generally, these trends have continued into the late 1980s; in 1986 70 per cent of married women aged 45-54 and 52 per cent of those aged 55-59 were deemed economically active (1986 *General Household Survey*, Table 8.8).

As with changing marriage patterns, the effects that increased labour market participation by married women might have on the community's capacity to care are not entirely clear. As Wicks (1982) has said, there is no suggestion 'that women in employment are unable or unwilling to care for elderly relatives'. However, he goes on to point out that, '... the decisions involved for such women are not easy and the pressures involved for those who combine the roles of wife, mother, worker and carer are often considerable ...' (p. 109).

Certainly, the evidence of the past 20 years suggests that women do combine the roles of carer and paid worker and that increased labour market participation has not significantly affected the likelihood of women being carers.

Hunt's survey in the mid-1960s (Hunt, 1968) found that 10 per cent of women in paid work and 12.5 per cent of women not in paid work 'were responsible for the care of at least one elderly or infirm person' (p. 109). However, women not in paid work were far more likely to be heavily involved in caring.

The most recent survey of women and employment (Martin and Roberts, 1984) has found that the proportion of all women caring for dependants, over and above looking after the family in the normal way, has risen since Hunt's survey (from 11 per cent to 13 per cent). Moreover, there was still little difference between the proportion of women who were in paid employment and providing care (13 per cent) and the proportion of those not in paid employment and providing care (15 per cent).

Similarly, the 1985 GHS has shown that around 17 per cent of married women in paid work are carers compared with around 20 per cent of those not (figures reworked from Green, 1988, Table 2.9). However, this survey also shows that women who were part-time workers were more likely to be carers than those working full-time, regardless of their marital status.

Thus, despite increased rates of participation in the labour market, women do no less caring than in the past; indeed, it seems that they do more. Paid employment outside the home appears to have very little effect on the extent of caring responsibility taken on. This suggests that increased participation in the labour market by married women should not necessarily be seen, as it has been by some commentators, as a 'threat' to the informal caring capacity of the community. Clearly some women do give up work when they would prefer to continue. Others are unable to work when they would like to and others choose or have to work as well as care. This topic is covered in more detail in Chapter 3. Further, as will be shown in Chapter 2, men and elderly people are rather more involved in caring than has previously been suspected. Arguments about the impact of women of working age on the capacity of the community to care thus need to be recast.

Summary and Conclusions

In the future there are clearly going to be larger numbers of people aged 75 and over living in the community and, because of the relationship between age, sex and disability, it seems that there will be a concomitant increase in the numbers requiring special care. This alone, ignoring any increase in numbers of children or working-age adults with disabilities, will increase pressure on the caring capacity of families and the 'community'. However, the assumption that increasing age will necessarily always imply a large and long degree of dependency should perhaps not go unchallenged. It may only be at the very end of life that most elderly people need intensive support from formal and informal sources (Wenger, 1984). Moreover, some would argue that it is society itself which creates some of the dependencies of old age and disability (Walker, 1981 and 1983), especially those that are financial in origin (Johnson, 1983). If elderly people had sufficient resources to purchase the care they required, as and when they needed it, then clearly they would not be 'dependent' in the sense that most commentators currently understand it. In addition, we do not know what effect recent changes in attitudes towards health (e.g. increased exercise, changed diet) and medical advances will have on dependency levels in future populations.

It does seem that there may, in the future, be fewer people available to take on responsibility for the care of dependents. Certainly more elderly people will be without family who might care for them. However, the state has always intervened with this group by providing some form of substitute care. It must be assumed that the state will continue this substitution, although alternative or cheaper methods of doing so are being sought (eg the Kent Community Care project, see Chapter 4).

It is also the case that, where families exist, there will be fewer members in them to take on the responsibilities of care for a dependant. However, as will be shown later, care is very rarely shared among family members at present. One individual has usually been responsible in the past; one individual will, presumably, be responsible in the future. The ratio of carers to cared for thus seems unlikely to change, although the probability that any one individual will become a main carer will increase. Finally, it is clear that, while the proportion of married women who are in paid employment has increased, this has not yet led to any reduction in the population of potential carers. Whether it does so in the future remains to be seen. Evidence to be presented in Chapter 2 suggests that it will not.

Chapter 2 # Who Cares?

Introduction

One of the most persistent misconceptions about 'modern society' is that the family no longer cares for its dependants, especially the elderly. Yet, as Brody (1981) has pointed out:

> 'research during the past several decades has systematically disproved the notion that contemporary families are alienated from the aged and do not take care of them as used to be the case in the "good old days". The accumulated evidence documents the strength of intergenerational behaviour, the frequency of contacts between generations, the predominance of families rather than professionals in the provision of health and social services, the strenuous family efforts to avoid institutional placement of the old, and the central role played by families in caring for the non-institutionalized impaired elderly.'

Unfortunately, as Brody continues, though science has signed the death certificate of 'family alienation from older people' the popular misunderstanding has eluded burial. So successful has this elusion been that another commentator (Shanas, 1979) has likened the misconception to 'a hydra-headed monster'.

The aim of this section is to identify clearly where care is usually based, who does the caring, why caring is mostly carried out by women and who 'ought' to care. Information about the extent of residential or institutional care for elderly people and for children and adults with disabilities is reviewed; the extent to which families and others are involved in the day-to-day care of dependent people is documented; and those within the family who bear the major responsibility for care are identified. Evidence on the role of women as carers and on who 'should' care for dependent people is also included.

The Locus of Care

Expectations and assumptions about where care for dependants should take place and who should undertake it vary with the type of dependant. Family responsibility for care of elderly people is, in most cases, assumed by off-spring after they have led a 'normal life' (Moroney, 1976). For families with a disabled child the position is radically different:

> 'Families, especially parents, are not faced with the prospect of providing care for a matter of years after a "normal life" but for decades. For these families the idea of a normal life has to be redefined.' (Moroney, 1976, p. 64)

While there is, in theory, an element of choice over whether or not an adult child assumes responsibility for an ageing parent, society rarely sanctions the same degree of choice for a parent in regard to his or her young children. Moreover, as shown in Chapter 1, many elderly people have no family who might take on responsibility for their care; this is true of only a very small proportion of children with disabilities. For adults with disabilities the issues are different again. Adults who *acquire* disabilities after a normal life might expect, and be expected by others, to continue to live where and with whom they were living while in full health. By contrast, young people with congenital disabilities or disabilities acquired in childhood, especially where these are physical and not mental impairments, might hope to leave home and establish an independent life in much the same way as their contemporaries. (Although it must be acknowledged that the reality of the situation is very different from this ideal, Hirst, 1984).

Expectations for adults with mental handicaps are less clear cut. In the past, certainly, there has been an implicit expectation that they could not live independent lives and, consequently, that where not in institutional care they should remain with their families. Indeed the 1971 White Paper *Better Services for the Mentally Handicapped* (Cmnd 4683), assumed that each handicapped person should live with his own family as long as this did not impose an undue burden on the family or on the handicapped person. The report of the Jay Committee (1979) (Cmnd 7468) challenged this assumption, however, proposing that 'the family should *not* be regarded as the central agent in the care and support [of a mentally handicapped person] until the parents are old and infirm'. It was suggested instead that 'a range of accommodation should be available which would allow the handicapped person to choose with his family whether to move out and establish a life independent of the parental home' (Wertheimer, 1981, p. 168-9).

Moves towards 'normalisation' of the lives of people with mental handicaps have also prompted questions about where they should live:

> '... if we say that mentally-handicapped people have the same rights as other people in British society does that not include the right to leave home at eighteen?' (Wertheimer, 1981, p. 169)

That 'society' holds these differing expectations about the locus of care for different dependency groups is given some empirical confirmation by two recent research projects, one carried out in Aberdeen (West et al., 1983 and 1984; West, 1984) and the other based on a national sample. In the Scottish study, 727 adults in three separate locations were asked to study vignettes of people of different ages and different types of disability. They were then asked to indicate which of several possible care arrangements should be adopted for each 'vignette'. In all cases the options ranged 'from family and informal care only (including the possibility of transfer to close kin) through domiciliary professional support, community based professional care [eg a day centre] to residential care of a partial or total kind'. Table 2.1 summarises the results of this study.

Table 2.1 Advocated care preference for the physically and mentally impaired of different ages (percentages)

Advocated care preference	Young (school leaver) physical	Young (school leaver) mental	Adult physical	Adult mental	Elderly physical	Elderly mental
Family and informal care *only*	20.2	16.0	29.3	44.8	14.8	9.2
Domiciliary professional help	17.7	9.0	28.7	16.4	17.7	7.4
Community based professional care	29.2	43.0	38.8	24.8	58.1	17.3
Residential care	33.0	32.0	2.2	14.0	9.5	66.0
Base (100%)	713	721	711	721	718	715

NB Both the adult and elderly 'mental impairment' vignettes related to psychiatric conditions rather than mental handicap.

Source: West et al., 1983, 1984.

The authors conclude that there is a consensus for care arrangements which can be 'termed community based professional care — day care centres, day hospitals, and notably in respect of elderly physical disability, sheltered housing', ie community rather than institutional care. However, it is also pointed out that:

> 'the public are discriminating. Their advocated preferences are strongly associated with the nature of the medical problem and the implications entailed for the (vignette) carers and dependants. This varies from relatively strong support for family and informal care in the psychiatric case, the only occasion this option is relatively preferred, to overwhelming support for residential care in respect of the confused elderly. There is evidence in the young and more particularly elderly dependency groups that mental impairment is more strongly associated with advocacy of professional involvement than physical impairment'. (West et al., 1984)

Although this research found little difference between the three samples in their expressed preferences, or between age groups or socio-economic groups, they did find that preferences differed slightly between men and women:

> 'In respect of sex ... there [was] a statistically significant difference between males and females in regard to both young mental and physical handicap and elderly physical disability. In these cases, women less often advocate family and informal care alone and more often prefer community based professional care options'. (ibid.)

This finding is, of course, important because, as will be shown below, it is women who shoulder the major burden of informal care.[1]

1. This effect was not, however, consistent over dependency groups and it seems more than likely that marital status, age and sex of the respondents would be interactive. For example, one could speculate that elderly married women would differ in their preferences for different dependency groups from, say, young adult single men. Unfortunately, the Aberdeen study could not explore these issues.

Another Scottish study (Weeks, undated), which questioned middle-aged people about preferences for their own care in old age, revealed that only a minority expected their families to look after them when they became old. A substantial majority 'had favourable attitudes towards being looked after in nursing homes or residential homes'.

Recent work in America has shown how age, or more correctly life-cycle status, is related to differing attitudes about, and preferences for, the locus of care for elderly people. A study of elderly women, their middle-aged daughters and young adult grand-daughters documented quite substantial differences between the groups (Brody, 1981; Davis, 1981). Grand-daughters 'felt more strongly than the middle generation and much more strongly than the grandmothers about ... "grandfilial responsibility", that is, that older people should expect help from their grandchildren' (Brody, 1987). While grandmothers strongly endorsed family care of the elderly they 'were more likely (75 per cent) than the daughters (61 per cent) and grand-daughters (59 per cent) to favour paying someone for ... care rather than obliging a working daughter to leave her job' to take on responsibility.

In addition, 'grandmothers were least likely to think that adult children with their own families should do household tasks for their parents' (Brody, 1981).

When the researchers asked questions which focused less on what people in general should do and more on what the individual women would like for themselves, they found that 'middle-generation' women were less likely than either the grandmothers [or] grand-daughters to prefer an adult child as provider of housework and personal care services'. The authors suggested that these preferences reflected the pressure of multiple responsibilities that the middle-generation women were feeling themselves or observing in their contemporaries.

While the majority of people in these studies saw the family and other informal settings as the right locus of care for dependants, very few felt that families should be left to cope alone and most saw an active role for the state in the provision of professional support and care. At the same time it was clear from the Scottish study that different mixes of care were felt appropriate for different types of dependency. Another important point, although not discussed by the authors, is that while there was a degree of consensus about the locus of care it was not complete. Individual differences are important; just as those cared for will have different preferences about where and by whom they should be cared for, so those doing the caring will have differing preferences.

New work by Janet Finch and Jennifer Mason (Finch, 1987) looks set to make a substantial contribution to knowledge in this area.

Does the Family Care?

Elderly people

Misconceptions about the abrogation of family responsibilities are, perhaps, strongest in relation to elderly people. Yet, while it is certainly true that the absolute number of elderly people in residential care has grown over the past 20 years, the proportion who are so cared for has not; only a tiny minority are in residential care and, moreover, the proportion in such care has not risen significantly since the turn of the century.

In 1985 it was estimated that there were approximately 4.3 million disabled people aged 60 years or over in Great Britain, of whom only 8 per cent were living in residential or institutional care (including long-stay hospitals). When applied to the total population of elderly people these figures suggest that around 0.4 per cent of those aged 60-69 and 1.3 per cent of those aged 70-79 were in residential care. Even among those aged 80 and over the proportion rises to only 4 per cent (figures derived from Tables 3.3 and 3.4, Martin, Meltzer and Elliot, 1988). By comparison, in 1900 2.8 per cent of the population of 70 and over, and in 1920 1.6 per cent of those aged 65 and over, were in public care (Halsey, 1972, Table 12.4).

A related misconception, about elderly people who do not live in residential care, is that they are neglected by their families to a greater degree than in the past. This misconception arises in part, perhaps, from the increasing number and proportions of elderly people who live alone. In 1961, 7.0 per cent of all households in Great Britain were elderly people living alone; by 1971 this proportion had risen to 12 per cent, and in 1987 was 16 per cent of all households (*Social Trends* 1989, Table 2.3). As indicated in Chapter 1, at least part of this increase is accounted for by the increase in childless marriages and a fall in the birth rate generally.

However, living alone does not necessarily mean that an elderly person is without support from his or her family, where one exists. As early as 1948, Sheldon's study of elderly people in Wolverhampton showed that widowed people often decided to live alone, rather than move in with family members because relatives, usually children, lived close at hand (Sheldon, 1948, p. 154). A large representative study of elderly people in the community (not in residential care) in the 1970s (Hunt, 1978) discovered just under a third living alone, although this proportion increased with age. However, when people did live alone support was often available from relatives. For example, shopping for bedfast or housebound elderly people was done by relatives in almost half the cases reported (Hunt, 1978, section 10.12 and Table 10.13.1).

Even among elderly people suffering from dementia, whom one might expect to be receiving hospital or institutional care, family care appears to be more important than formal care (Kay et al., 1970; Bergmann et al., 1978; Isaacs et al., 1972).

Most recently the 1986 General Household Survey (OPCS 1989) has shown that 20 per cent of men and 48 per cent of women aged 65 or over live alone. However, 84 per cent of all those aged 65 and over said that they saw relatives or friends at least once a week, 33 per cent every or nearly every day. By contrast, only 2 per cent said that they never saw relatives or friends (OPCS, 1989, Table 12.23). Among those who lived alone the proportions seeing relatives or friends at least weekly was even higher — 89 per cent — with 43 per cent seeing them every or nearly every day. Only 2 per cent of those living alone said that they saw no one 'nowadays' (Table 12.26).

As in Hunt's study, the GHS revealed that when elderly people were unable to carry out domestic tasks for themselves relatives were the usual sources of help. For example, 11 of the 15 per cent of all elderly people unable to do their own shopping received help from relatives and another 2 per cent from friends, while 7 of the 11 per cent who could not sweep or clean floors, and 6 of the 7 per cent who could not cook a main meal, had help from family members. Even among those who lived alone it was only in relation to heavy domestic tasks such as cleaning paintwork, windows and floors that help from formal or paid sources exceeded that from the informal sources of family and friends.

While it is difficult to draw any conclusions about changes in the pattern of family care for elderly people from the studies reviewed here — they are based on dissimilar samples from dissimilar communities — there is no apparent evidence of wholesale abrogation of responsibility by families. The provision of statutory services to elderly people has certainly increased since 1948 but this has largely been to support elderly people without families close by rather than replace or supplement family care (Bergmann et al., 1978; Moroney, 1976; Arber et al., 1988). Indeed, it can be argued that care of elderly people by their families may be more common now than in the past. Johnson and Johnson (cited in Greengross, 1982) have suggested that today's 'modified extended families' care more extensively and for longer than ever before. As more elderly people live to a very old age it is inevitable, then, that a greater proportion of the next generation will become responsible for their care.

Children with disabilities

In 1971 the DHSS paper *Better services for the mentally handicapped* (HMSO 1971, Cmnd. 4683) estimated that slightly over 70 per cent of children with severe mental handicaps were living with their families. However, it was obvious even at this stage that policies encouraging care in the community for people with mental handicaps were beginning to have an impact. The number of children resident in NHS hospitals in England, Scotland and Wales in 1976 was 4,879 (Cmnd. 7468), a population some 4,405 lower than in 1970. In addition, in 1977, 1,721 children with disabilities were living in local authority homes but this represented an increase of only 300 or so since 1970.

Most recently the OPCS disablement surveys have shown how few children with disabilities live in residential or institutional care compared with the number who live in private households. Bone and Meltzer (1989) suggest that, while some 360,000 children with disabilities live in Great Britain, there are only 5,600 or so (about 1.5 per cent of the total) in long-term residential or institutional care. Children with disabilities related to behaviour, communication or intellectual functioning were more likely to be in residential establishments than were children with other types of disability. Older children (ten years or more) and boys were more likely to be in residential care than were younger children or girls.

All the available evidence, then, points to a small, and declining, proportion of children with disabilities being cared for away from private households.

That the majority of children with severe disabilities are cared for by their families 'in the community' does not, however, mean that the community at large is involved in their care. The question of who is actually involved in providing care is discussed later in this chapter.

Adults with mental handicaps

Of the groups so far considered, adults with mental handicaps seem to be most likely to be in some form of institutional or residential care. Bayley's (1973) study of all the people with mental handicaps registered with the Sheffield Mental Health Service in 1968 showed quite clear differences in age structure between those still at home and those who had been admitted to institutional or residential care. Although around two-thirds of all those with severe mental handicaps were living at home, this proportion dropped with age.

Estimates in the early 1970s (HMSO, 1971, Cmnd. 4683) suggested that over a half of severely mentally handicapped adults did not live with their own families. Trends towards a reduction of the number of long-stay residents in mental handicap hospitals will obviously have had an impact here. However, at least some of this change will have been accommodated by the growth in the number of places in local authority, private and voluntary hostels and 'homes', from a total of around 12,000 in 1976 to 24,000 in 1986 in England alone (DoH, 1988, Table 7.3). People with mental handicaps will thus have been transferred from one form of residential care to another.

The OPCS disablement surveys suggest that in the mid-1980s around 35 per cent of the population of adults whose disabilities were caused by mental handicaps were living in residential establishments (calculated from Tables 3.1, 4.3, and 4.10, Martin, Meltzer and Elliot, 1988).

This apparent reduction in the proportion of people with mental handicaps who are living in long-stay residential care may represent a real drop in the numbers who experience this form of care. However, the reduction could also be accounted for by admission at a later stage than before, rather than not being admitted at all (see Moroney, 1976).

Adults with physical disabilities and chronic illnesses

It is extremely difficult to estimate the proportion of non-elderly people with physical disabilities who are living in institutional or residential care, although, as indicated earlier in this section, one would probably expect both the proportion and the numbers to be small. The OPCS disablement surveys contain no overall classification of 'physical disability' but rather classify a whole series of disabilities, any of which may or may not be associated with other forms of disability. Thus, for example, someone with a disability of locomotion may also have a disability of intellectual functioning associated with mental handicap. Table 2.2, below, shows the estimated proportions of non-elderly people (under the age of 60) with different types of disabilities who were living in residential establishments when the OPCS surveys were carried out.

Table 2.2 Proportions of estimated population of non-elderly adults with different types of disability living in residential establishments

Type of disability	% of estimated population living in residential care
Locomotion	3.5
Reaching and stretching	6.2
Dexterity	5.0
Seeing	15.7
Hearing	6.1
Personal care	7.9
Continence	9.2
Communication	12.8
Behaviour	7.1
Intellectual functioning	9.4
Consciousness	13.3
Eating, drinking, digestion	12.8
Disfigurement	not available

Derived from Table 3.13, Martin, Meltzer and Elliot, 1988

Broadly speaking, the table suggests that people with physical types of disability (locomotion, dexterity, reaching and stretching) were substantially less likely to be in residential establishments than were people with types of disability often associated with mental impairment (communication, intellectual functioning, consciousness). However, for the reasons already outlined, this does not give a very accurate guide to the proportion of adults who have physical disabilities *only* who live in residential care.

There are substantial hints in other literature relating to disablement about the high incidence of family care for people with physical disabilities and chronic illnesses. For example, a study of young adults (Hirst, 1982) has shown how few are able to move away from home and establish independent lives in the same way as their contemporaries.

In a study by Cartwright (1973) only 9 per cent of a sample of 785 people (including some elderly people) who had recently died, had been in a hospital or institution for the 12 months before their death. A similar proportion (8 per cent) of Sainsbury's (1970) original sample of adults on local authority disability registers were living in residential establishments or hospitals. None of Blaxter's (1976) sample of non-elderly adults with a disability went to live in residential care when discharged from hospital and, it appears, all were still in their own homes a year later.

Among men with a spinal cord injury (Creek et al., not dated) it seems that rather a higher proportion may be initially discharged into some form of residential care. However, at the time of interview, between a year and 14 years since the original injury, only 3 per cent were still in some form of residential or institutional care.

Perhaps the nearest we can get to a reasonably accurate estimate is via figures on occupancy of local authority, voluntary and private residential establishments. In 1986 there were 15,645 adults under 65 years with only physical disabilities in this type of accommodation (DoH, 1988, Table 7.1). This represents less than 1 per cent of the *total* estimated population of non-elderly population with disabilities.

Even with these imperfect approximations it is clear that long-term residential care plays very little part in the care of non-elderly adults with physical disabilities.

Who cares within the family?

We have seen that the majority of children and adults within the dependency groups considered in the review live 'in the community', rather than in any form of residential care. Although the proportions of each dependency group who live with relatives vary, the family is still the most important locus of care for all of them. However, to talk about 'care by the community' or even 'family' care is to disguise the reality. In fact, as is shown in the following sub-sections, 'care by the community' almost always means care by family members with little support from others in 'the community'. Further, it appears that shared care between family members is uncommon; once one person has been identified as the main carer other relatives withdraw. However, the extent to which particular relatives or others are involved in the care of dependent people varies both between dependency groups and also within, influenced, as one might predict, by where and with whom the dependent person lives.

When the first edition of this book was published in 1985 evidence from the available research literature suggested that 'care by family members almost always means care by female members with little support from other relatives' (Parker, 1985, p. 30). Since then, re-analysis of the 1980 GHS and the publication of both the 1985 GHS and the OPCS disablement surveys have raised questions about this assumption, especially in relation to elderly people. It is now clear that far more men are involved in providing care than was previously believed but that much of this is accounted for by men looking after their wives. Until very recently (Parker, 1989a) spouses had not really been a focus of attention in informal care research, which may account for the lack of recognition of the part men may play. These findings underline again the importance of taking into account who is being cared for, where, and with whom they live when asking the question 'who cares?'.

Elderly people

The majority of elderly people live either alone (20 per cent of men, 48 per cent of women) or with their spouse (62 per cent men, 33 per cent women) and only relatively small proportions live with others (1986 GHS). Consequently we can see that, if and when elderly people become in need of care, where and by whom it is provided is likely to vary substantially.

When studies have concentrated on elderly people who are cared for by relatives of a younger generation (usually offspring) it has been found that daughters and daughters-in-law are most heavily involved. Both

Sheldon (1948) and Townsend (1957) found that elderly people were more likely to live with a married daughter than with a married son. Similarly, daughters and daughters-in-law were more likely to be helping elderly people with household and other tasks than were sons and sons-in-law in Hunt's (1978) study of old people at home. Only in the matter of visiting elderly people did male children help to anywhere near the same extent as female children.

More recently, Nissel and Bonnerjea (1982), in their exploration of the ways in which caring for elderly relatives constrains 'women's participation in the community', have underlined the heavy burden borne by women caring for elderly relatives. Husbands rarely gave direct help to their wives with the care of the dependent relative living with them, even where the wife was employed outside the home. The majority 'gave the impression of being quite distant from the situation. Many of them denied there were any serious problems ...' (p. 35).

Among elderly mentally ill people, where the stresses of care are even greater, women also bear the brunt of responsibility when caring for parents (Isaacs et al, 1972, Sandford, 1975, Levin et al, 1983).

In a study of the carers of people suffering from senile dementia (Gilhooly, 1982), it was found that expectations among family members influenced who cared: '... when there were both sons and daughters who could potentially give assistance sons were rarely expected to give as much help as daughters'.

Daughters and daughters-in-law become the main carers for elderly people not because they are necessarily the only people available to take on the task. Many researchers have identified that often 'one person in the family [is] singled out to carry more than a fair share of the burden of care' (Townsend, 1957).

Nissel and Bonnerjea (1982) noted that 'once the relative was settled with one of his/her children, the other "children" contributed very little. This caused growing resentment as the relative needed more and more attention, and as the carer had less and less time for her previous work and other activities' (p. 32). Similar patterns are evident from Gilhooly's work: 'It seemed that once one person had formally taken on the responsibility of care, the rest stopped helping at all' and '... "family" care means care by *one* member of the family. It was exceedingly rare to find cases of real "shared" caregiving. In those few cases of genuine shared caregiving it was a son and his wife, never the dependent's daughter and her husband' (Gilhooly, 1982).

While it is true that the sex of the potential carer does determine to a large extent who actually takes on that role, it is also the case that the nature of the kinship tie plays a part. Qureshi and Simons (1987) have demonstrated the existence of 'a systematic set of rules for deciding [who should care for elderly people] between available network members' (p. 129). Both kinship obligations and gender interact to produce a hierarchy of expectation or obligation: spouse, daughter, daughter-in-law, son, other relatives, non-relatives. (This hierarchy alerts us again to the important role of spouses, to which we shall turn later.)

Further, Qureshi and Walker (forthcoming) suggest that co-residence also has a part to play in determining who becomes a carer for an elderly person. Thus single off-spring, who never leave home or who marry but return after divorce or separation, may be more likely to become carers for their parents than off-spring who live away, regardless of their sex. The importance of co-residence is given further weight by findings from Glendinning's recent qualitative work (Glendinning, 1989). As one might expect from Qureshi and Walker's 'hierarchy', when elderly people who need care are still living with their marital or quasi-marital partner, it is the spouse who is most likely to be the carer. Indeed, recent evidence makes it quite obvious that spouses are the most important group of carers for elderly people as a whole. However, widespread acknowledgement of this fact has taken some time in coming.

In 1983 Levin et al expressed surprise at the proportion of confused elderly people in their study (40 per cent) who were supported by their spouses while in 1984 Wenger concluded that 'informal carers, particularly elderly spouses, apparently provide the bulk of support for the frail elderly at home' in a rural community (Wenger, 1984, p. 117). In an urban community Qureshi and Simons (1987), found that, in half of the cases in the elderly population studied who had an 'identified within-household' helper, this helper was a spouse.

Re-analysis of the 1980 GHS (Evandrou et al., 1986) has shown that more than nine out of ten elderly married people who need help with domestic and personal self-care tasks receive it from their spouse. Further, the re-analysis indicated that almost a third of 'severely disabled' elderly people lived in households as couples with just their spouse and that such couples 'were almost exactly equally divided between those in which the wife is caring for the husband and those in which the husband is caring for the wife' (Arber and Gilbert, 1989).

Given these findings, it should, perhaps, not be so surprising that the 1985 GHS (Green, 1988) revealed so many men who identified themselves as 'having extra responsibilities because they look[ed] after someone who is sick, handicapped or elderly' (1985 GHS interview schedule).

In sum, then, it can now be seen that patterns of care-giving for elderly people are more complex than earlier work on informal care suggested. As Arber and Gilbert (1989) have summed it up:

> '... the gender balance of co-resident caring for the elderly differs according to four types of kin relationship: (a) caring as part of a marital relationship — men and women are equally likely to care for an elderly spouse, (b) a filial relationship involving an unmarried carer — slightly fewer unmarried sons than unmarried daughters care for an elderly parent, (c) a sibling relationship — elderly sisters are much more likely to be carers than brothers, and (d) a filial relationship involving a married carer — [it is assumed] that men are unlikely to be carers.' (p. 113)

It is, of course, still the case that women make up the majority of those who care for elderly people in the community. In addition, it is women who are most likely to take up responsibilities for care outside the bounds of marriage, i.e. for parents or siblings.

Children with disabilities

By contrast with the evidence about care of elderly people, recent research has done little to challenge the analysis presented in the first edition of this book about the care of children with disabilities. As in the great majority of families with children, the bulk of caring for a disabled child is done by his or her mother with little help from other family members.

Wilkin (1979) found that large proportions of mothers caring for children with mentally handicapped children received no help with child care. Neither was any help with basic domestic tasks given. The 'majority of mothers carried a very heavy burden with very little support' (p. 118). The father's role in most families 'varied little from the dominant cultural pattern' yet 'most could have and should have done more to ease the burden on their wives' (pp. 129, 133).

Wilkin also concluded that his study: 'cast considerable doubt on the importance which should be attached to networks [of kin, friends and neighbours] as sources of support with the daily routine of child care and housework' (p. 195).

Glendinning (1983), in her in-depth study of 17 families with severely mentally and/or physically disabled children, while acknowledging that fathers did not take as much responsibility for the day-to-day child care as did mothers, felt that objective measures or assessments of the fathers' participation were probably less important in mediating mothers' stress than their *perceived* willingness to help.

Older children were often, but not invariably, 'an important source of practical support' to the families in Glendinning's study. None of the families had substantial regular or frequent practical help from other family members outside the household. 'Relatives' own family commitments or grandparents' advancing age meant that some parents just did not expect any help' (p. 99), while others recognised family members' reluctance to offer help because of 'their apprehension about medical, nursing or behaviour problems' which might arise. Practical help from neighbours was similarly limited.

In Glendinning's more recent study (Glendinning, 1985) fathers' involvement with child care was found to be greater than might have been expected but was concentrated on the more pleasurable and less tasking activities such as playing with or amusing the child. Around 44 per cent of the families who had relatives living nearby received practical help from them on a regular basis and just under two-thirds received some emotional or moral support. Less than a third of families had regular practical help from friends and neighbours, and under a half received any moral support.

Almost identical conclusions can be drawn from other recent studies of carers of mentally handicapped children (for example Carey, 1982; Ayer and Alaszewski, 1984).

Carey concludes, as did Wilkin, that fathers' contributions to household duties and child care were insufficient to 'support the conclusion that role relationships in handicapped families are approaching symmetry'.

Results from the more broadly based Child Health and Education Study (Cooke, 1982) reinforce scepticism about sharing of child care and housework in families with a disabled child. While 88 per cent of fathers spent some time during the week keeping children amused at home, only 42 per cent ever took the children out without their mother at least once or twice a week. Help with domestic tasks was at an even lower level overall. Under a half helped with shopping at least once or twice a week and around a third helped to clean the house or with the cooking. The only 'substantial' contribution was made with washing up; just under two-thirds of husbands helped with this at least once or twice a week. The lowest level of help was given with washing (12 per cent) and ironing (6 per cent).

Help with household tasks did not appear to increase with severity of the child's disability:

'the tendency was for greater severity of handicap to be associated with slightly greater participation in child care and slightly less participation in housework. However, in general it was mothers who bore the main burden of responsibility' (p. 71)

A study of the family life of children with cystic fibrosis in Northern Ireland (Burton, 1975) has produced a picture of family care and support somewhat at variance with those painted by the other studies reported here. While the mothers were most closely involved in giving therapy to the children (mothers devoted an average of five hours a week to this on top of their normal domestic duties compared to fathers' 45 minutes a week), it seemed that they had considerable support from both family and community. Mothers who managed to work outside the home 'often substituted the care of relatives and domestics for their own care'. Additional domestic help was available to most mothers, usually coming from their immediate family. 'From the spontaneous comments of most mothers, it was obvious that family members were a great source of strength and practical assistance offering whatever services were required' (p. 122). Only 9 per cent of the mothers had no such support available; all of these were recent immigrants to Northern Ireland. In addition, 50 per cent of all mothers accepted occasional help from friends or neighbours.

It is not entirely clear why the mothers in Burton's study should have been apparently better supported than mothers in the other studies. However it seems that cultural factors may have been important. Certainly, as already indicated, recent arrivals in Northern Ireland did not have the same support network available to them as did mothers who were native to the province.

At first sight the evidence from the studies reviewed in this section seems at variance with that presented in the 1985 GHS report on informal care (Green, 1988). In this it is revealed that of those caring for a dependant in the same household 8 per cent of the men and 12 per cent of the women said that they were looking after a child under the age of 16. However, a closer look at the report shows that women caring for a child[1] in the same household were much more likely than men to say that

1. The relevant table (5.2, Green, 1988) aggregates figures for all those caring for a child, regardless of the child's age.

no-one else helped them to look after their dependant. This difference was much greater (25 per cent compared to 8 per cent) than it was in any other sub-group of same-household carers. Further, it seems likely that additional analysis will reveal other differences. For example, preliminary reanalysis by Lawton and Parker (forthcoming) shows that 61 per cent of women caring for disabled or sick children spend at least 50 hours a week doing so, compared with 36 per cent of men. Again, this is a larger difference than any found in other sub-groups of carers.

In summary then, the major share of caring for children with disabilities or chronic illnesses falls to mothers, with relatively little help from fathers, siblings, relatives, neighbours or friends. A major problem associated with these studies is, however, the inadequate way in which 'help' is measured. Wilkin (1979) identified this problem when he contrasted his finding, that the mothers of mentally handicapped children received little support from families and neighbours, with earlier studies (Bayley, 1973; Carr, 1976; Burton, 1975) which apparently demonstrated the availability of considerable support. This, he felt, was due to none of the other studies having: '... systematically collected information about what individuals actually did with respect to a wide range of domestic tasks' (p. 145).

Non-elderly adults with disabilities

One of the difficulties with the major sources of information about the care of non-elderly dependent adults is that they are not exclusive in their scope. Harris (1971) included both physically and mentally impaired people and elderly and non-elderly people in her survey. Similarly, the subjects in Cartwright's (1973) research about the 12 months prior to death included both elderly and non-elderly people. Studies which are limited to specific types of disability and/or to non-elderly adults only tend to be small and consequently more limited in their applicability. Even in the recent OPCS disablement surveys, as we have already seen, it is often difficult to distinguish between adults with physical disabilities alone and others. Further, the sections in the survey which report findings on informal care do not always distinguish between elderly and non-elderly adults. These limitations should be borne in mind in the rest of this sub-section.

Adults with mental handicaps

Perhaps because so many adults with mental handicaps have, in the past, been cared for in institutional accommodation of one form or another, their care in the community does not appear to have attracted as much attention from researchers as has the care of children.

In-depth interviews with families caring for mentally handicapped adults in Sheffield revealed a very low level of support for the mothers of these people (Bayley, 1973). Only 14 out of the 36 fathers interviewed in the study helped 'much' with the care of their mentally handicapped son or daughter. Siblings still at home helped even less, but this was often as a result of deliberate policy on the parent's part. In 16 out of 50 cases other relatives were said to give 'much' help and support to the mother but it was more common for one relative, almost always a woman, to be of particular help than it was for there to be a wide spread of family helping. Neither was support from neighbours extensive, although some families preferred this. Some families desperately needed help but were unable, or found it difficult, to accept it.

Most families managed to develop some coping structure but this weakened as the mentally handicapped person and his parents aged. When other children left the parental home a source of help departed with them. When they had children of their own the amount of help they might be able to offer diminished still further. In general, however, the 'coping structure' depended on one person, nearly always a mother. Consequently the most likely reason for breakdown of care was the death or illness of that person.

A recent study, in which the carers of 353 mentally handicapped adults in West Yorkshire were interviewed (City of Bradford MDC Social Services Department, 1983), identified both main and secondary carers. The findings are reproduced in Table 2.3.

Table 2.3 Main and secondary carers of mentally handicapped adults living at home

	Main carer	Secondary carer
Mother	80	3
Father	9	49
Sibling	6	4
Spouse	1	—
Other relative	4	8
No carer	—	36
Total (100%)	352	352

One male subject was not included in these figures as he was himself caring for his elderly, infirm mother.

Source: City of Bradford MDC Social Services Department 1983.

The average age of main carers in this study was 57 (although the range was wide, from 20 to 86 years); 41 per cent of them were aged 60 or over. The secondary carers were of a similar average age and range.

Even though the researchers did not explore the inter-relationships between main and secondary carers and household composition (indeed, no information on household composition is included in the report), it can be seen that just over a third of the main carers had no support from household members or others. Even if one assumed that there was no secondary support for any of the main carers, *except* mothers, this would still leave nearly 20 per cent of the mothers without secondary support.

Another study of mentally handicapped people (including some children), living in rural and remote areas of Scotland, discovered that in households with only one parent the presence of, particularly, grandmothers appeared to be important in keeping the mentally handicapped family member at home (Seed, 1980). Support from relatives outside the household was noted in two-thirds of the social networks studied but there were 'more instances of contacts with relatives in the case of mentally handicapped children than adults' (p.

47). Families with little or no contact with relatives did not appear to compensate for this by other social contacts.

Adults with physical disabilities and illnesses

The majority of adults with physical disabilities, who are not in residential care, appear to live with family members. Harris's (1971) survey (which did contain some people with mental handicaps) showed that only 9.4 per cent of adults aged 16-64, who were handicapped or impaired, lived by themselves. The majority lived with their spouse and/or children, others with parents or siblings, and a few with unrelated people. Most, then, lived in households where, in theory, others were available to help care for them.

Sainsbury (1970) found that 16 per cent of those under pension age, in a group of registered disabled adults, lived alone while 20 per cent still lived with their parents. Striking differences were evident in the patterns of help and support received by the disabled person, depending on the composition of their households. Thus only 26 per cent of those living alone received help from relatives while 84 per cent and 92 per cent, respectively, of those in two-person and three-or more person households did. However, very little of this help came from relatives *outside* the household. Indeed 'in spite of other relatives in the neighbourhood, where a disabled person required considerable help during the day, the burden of care was usually undertaken by one relative within the household' (p. 130).

In one-person households where relatives were providing support, the helper was most often a single relative, usually a daughter. Only where care was not available within the family did statutory services step into the breach. Only 16 per cent of all the households received help from neighbours although this type of help was more important to those living alone than to others.

Similar variation in source of help with household composition was evident in Cartwright's study of the 12 months preceding the deaths of a sample of elderly and non-elderly adults. Those who had been living only with their spouses before death (33 per cent of those under 65 years) had most often been helped by the spouse, while people living with relatives of a younger generation had been helped most often by their children or children-in-law.

There was usually (in 83 per cent of cases) one person who 'bore the brunt' of care even though others might be involved. Wives and husbands generally bore the brunt of caring for the married, daughters for the widowed, sisters and other relatives for the single. The 'brunt bearer' was 'almost always a family member (nine-tenths), and generally a woman (three-quarters)' (p. 155).

It was found that neighbours 'rarely undertook nursing care' although relatives often did so, indicating perhaps that there were certain personal tasks which it may be impossible to expect the 'community', rather than the family, to undertake (cf Wright, 1983).

In one study (Blaxter, 1976) non-elderly men discharged from hospital with a disability were most likely to have spouses not in paid employment at home to care for them. Fewer problems of personal care and daily living thus arose for them than for discharged women patients. Difficulties with personal care were mostly 'solved' by the care of 'daughters, or to a lesser extent sisters, mothers, other kinsfolk and neighbours' (p. 57). Neighbours 'were essential only if there were no female relatives available' (p. 57).

Family support in the city Blaxter studied seemed rather stronger than that reported in other studies. Some of this appeared to be due to expectations of the cared-for person or of professionals rather than of the carers. 'It appeared to be taken for granted by all that if female relatives were available, no problem could exist' (p. 58). In some cases, patients refused to contemplate alternative forms of outside help, expecting their, usually female, relatives to cope. Although the caring relatives appeared to take this duty for granted, for some it caused considerable hardship. Indeed this unquestioned assumption that mainly female family members would provide, when professionals colluded with it, led to 'some of the most obvious failures in ensuring necessary care'.

A study of people reliant on wheelchairs (Hyman, 1977) also emphasises the importance of family support for people with physical disabilities. Of the 56 people (all under the age of 65) who were interviewed, 31 were living with a spouse, ten with their parents, four with siblings or grown children, three with a friend or companion. Only eight were living alone. Further, when help was needed with daily living activities (29 of the sample), this was most often provided by a spouse (15 cases) or parents (nine cases). In only one case did someone who was not a relative help in this way. Similar patterns of help giving and the relative lack of involvement of adult children, other relatives or neighbours have been identified in recent research on non-elderly disabled adults (Parker, 1988 and 1989a).

Finally, the OPCS disablement survey has shown that 60 per cent of disabled adults (including elderly people) need help with at least one everyday activity and that the vast majority (56 per cent) receive this help from informal sources. Half of this group got this help from their spouse, 20 per cent from children within the household and 21 per cent from children outside the household. Only 13 per cent of disabled adults receiving any help from informal sources got it from a friend or neighbour living in another household (Martin, White and Meltzer, 1989). More specifically, 'over 90 per cent of those who needed more than occasional help [with self-care activities] received some informal help from a relative or friend' (p. 93), in most cases from someone in their household.

Summary and Conclusions

The evidence reviewed here shows, unequivocally, that families do care for their dependent relatives and that there has been no wholesale abrogation of family 'obligation' to care. The state has not taken over the care of dependent people who have families but has, rather, stepped in to support those who do not.

Despite recent recognition of the part that men might play in providing care, particularly to their elderly spouses, this chapter has demonstrated that it is still the case that, in the population at large, women provide the bulk of care. Further, on an individual level, women are more likely to be heavily involved in caring than are men. Thus there is little evidence of any real shift in the 'social division of community care' (Walker, 1982).

One of the most striking things to emerge from this chapter is, perhaps, the difference in care arrangements between sub-groups of people who need care and, consequently, the varying levels of involvement between different types of kin. This is an important issue and one which should inform both future research in this area, particularly in relation to secondary analysis of large-scale data sets, and future theoretical analysis, particularly in relation to alternative options to 'family' care.

Chapter 3

The Costs of Caring

Introduction

The costs to informal carers of caring for dependent people can include economic, physical, emotional and opportunity costs: loss and restriction of employment; reduced income; increased expenditure; restricted family and social life and physical and emotional strain, are all examples. Such effects may vary, depending on who is doing the caring and where. Moreover, while some effects may be uniform across dependency groups others, for example those relating to employment opportunities, may not.

As has been indicated, it is only relatively recently that research has focused explicitly on informal carers. Nowhere is this more true than in regard to thorough analysis of the costs of care. When the first edition of this review was written there were relatively few detailed accounts of the tasks carers undertake, the time taken up by caring, the true costs in lost income, increased expenditure, lost opportunities, and so on.

While this position has improved in regard to descriptions of what caring entails, it is still the case that the full economic costs (and indeed value) of informal caring remain to be calculated. Economists have recently turned their attention to the costs of 'community care', but such analysis has, with a few exceptions, concentrated on the relative costs of care in large institutions and care in smaller institutions or hostels 'in the community'. Where analysis has extended to the costs of community care in dependent people's own homes (Wright et al., 1981; Opit, 1977) costs to the State *only* have been considered, mainly because of the technical problems of gauging costs to informal carers (Chetwynd, 1983). Despite the fact that the economic advantage of community care, whether in a smaller institution or in the dependent person's own home, is not very great (Maynard and Smith, 1983) the belief has arisen that community care is necessarily cheaper than institutional care. This is not surprising when the transfer of costs from the formal to the informal sector has been almost completely ignored.

However, some progress has been made, most significantly, perhaps, by Baldwin (1985) and Joshi (1987), and that information will be reviewed here. In addition, information from recent, more qualitatively oriented research will be used to illustrate the impact which informal caring has on the lives of those who provide it.

There are at least three reasons why accurate assessment of the costs of informal caring is of interest. First, if policy is to be developed with the explicit aim of supporting informal carers, baselines need to be established from which the effect of supporting services can be measured. Secondly, it seems intuitively likely that there will be a relationship between the costs of caring and the quality of care given. Finally, it is likely that the length of time for which carers are able to continue caring will also be related to the costs caring imposes.

Before policies encouraging care in and by the community develop much further it seems essential that better information to illuminate these issues should be available. This section of the review covers what is known already, and points out what remains to be discovered, of the economic, physical and emotional costs of caring, covering, in turn, employment, income, expenditure, physical and emotional stress.

Employment

It might be expected that the impact of caring on employment outside the home would vary between dependency groups, mainly as a result of differences in main carers' ages and household circumstances. Children with disabilities are cared for by their relatively young mothers who, under normal circumstances, might expect to be economically active once their children are beyond early childhood. The carers of adults with disabilities, by contrast, fall into two groups. First, there are those for whom caring has always been a feature of their lives as their children grow from disabled children to disabled adults. Secondly, there are those whose lives have been disrupted when the person they care for acquired a disability during adulthood. Obviously, the effect of caring on employment for these categories of carers will be different even if the outcome (not having paid work outside the home) is the same. The carers of elderly people with dementia who become dependent at a relatively early age are likely to be in mid-career when responsibilities interrupt their work outside the home. By contrast, those caring for elderly people who are not mentally infirm are likely to be quite old themselves, whether of the same generation (spouses, siblings, friends), and thus beyond retirement or of a younger generation but approaching retirement age.

The effects of caring for a dependant are, of course, not confined to giving up or losing a job. Reduction of hours at work, fewer opportunities for overtime, restricted career development and promotion, and loss of pension rights may occur among carers able to continue working outside the home. These effects may also vary between groups of carers. The rest of this sub-section examines what is known about the impact of caring on carers' employment, taking elderly people, children, and adult dependants by turn.

Carers of elderly people

It is clear, from surveys of the family life of old people (Sheldon, 1948, Townsend, 1957), from studies of elderly people who are mentally infirm (Isaacs et al., 1972), from recent work which has concentrated on the carers of elderly people (Nissel and Bonnerjea, 1982; Wright, 1983; Levin et al., 1983; Bowling, 1984; Lewis and Meredith, 1988) and from surveys of women and employment (Hunt, 1968; Martin and Roberts, 1984), that younger relatives looking after old people do give up work in order to continue caring, or when they continue in paid employment, lose time at work.

A quarter of carers in an EOC survey (EOC, 1980) gave up work and lost or altered hours worked as a direct result of caring for elderly or disabled dependants. Others had foregone promotion and training opportunities. Nine of the 15 carers in Nissel and Bonnerjea's pilot study who were not in paid employment had given up their jobs because of their dependent relative and most would have liked to take up paid work again.

However, the relationship between paid work and caring is influenced by other factors in the carer's life. Lewis and Meredith (1988), in their qualitative study of 41 daughters who had cared for their mothers, show clearly how the impact of caring on employment varied with 'the daughter's stage in the life course and her expectations' (p. 37). If in early middle-age daughters, particularly those who were single, found it difficult to give up work and sacrifice pension entitlements. In later middle age, the daughters might opt for early retirement, a reduced workload, or a less demanding career path. Thus the younger daughters might carry a very heavy burden, providing substantial care while at the same time attempting to hold down a full-time job. This is an effect identified also by Isaacs et al. (1972), who pointed out that the majority of daughters in their survey were the only wage-earners in the household and thus 'dreaded the loss of their jobs if they stayed off work' (p. 66). These studies also show the importance of the carer's marital status in mediating the relationship between paid work and caring. This is underlined by Ungerson's (1987) recent study of 19 people caring for an elderly person, which indicated that some women were able to become 'career' carers only because their husband's were earning enough to support both them and the dependent elderly person. By contrast, single women, and women whose husbands did not have very large earnings, had little option but to combine paid work and caring.

The relationship between paid work, caring and stress (which will be dealt with in more detail later) is complex. For younger carers, at least, work outside the home can be beneficial. Gilhooly's study of those supporting elderly mentally infirm people showed that part-time work provided an 'emotional outlet' for female carers who could not have continued giving care without that outlet. Only a few of those who had managed to continue in paid employment said that they would give up work 'to enable the dementing relative to remain in the community'. However, even these carers said that they hoped the situation would never get 'that bad' (Gilhooly, 1986, p. 170). It seems likely that these respondents were expressing opinions about what they hoped would happen rather than about what might actually happen, because, as we have seen, women *do* give up their jobs to take on caring responsibilities. Further, at least some of them 'had ... to work for financial reasons' (ibid.).

However, as already suggested, combining paid employment with caring is not necessarily beneficial. Sheldon (1948) reported examples of 'severe hardship' among younger people caring for elderly parents while continuing in paid employment outside the home. This is even more the case for older carers. While employment might ideally make a welcome contribution to household income, the double strain of work and caring, without help from other sources, may be too great. An American study of wives of elderly disabled men (Fengler and Goodrick, 1979) suggests this:

> 'Although the involvement in a job would seem to have the advantage of getting the wife out of the household, this seems to be offset by the exhaustion that results from too many additional responsibilities'.

This last study also alerts us to the fact that elderly people are not always cared for by people of a younger generation. Indeed, as shown in Chapter 2, much of the care for this group is, in fact, provided by people of the same generation, most usually spouses. Consequently, the employment effects of providing care to elderly people are mostly confined to that proportion of carers who are younger than those they care for.

Carers of children with disabilities

Most studies of childhood disability have documented some impact on, especially, mothers' employment opportunities. While it is difficult to tease out from these studies the separate effects of social class, prevailing labour-market participation rates, and of social and cultural expectations, it does seem that the nature and severity of a child's disability are important determinants of mothers' ability to work outside the home.

Just over a third of mothers, in a study of children with cystic fibrosis (Burton, 1975), who were not in paid work outside the home, would have liked to seek employment but in very few cases did they feel that their child's illness prevented them from doing so. Of those in paid employment, only a quarter felt that caring for their ill child had ever caused any particular difficulties. Among mothers with mentally handicapped children, Wilkin (1979) found that 40 per cent were working outside the home, but 61 per cent overall would have liked to work or work longer hours if already in employment. By contrast, very few mothers of children who were *severely* mentally handicapped in another study (Bayley, 1973) had paid work. Twenty-three per cent of mothers whose children were still at home had paid employment, mostly part-time, but this was true of only 9 per cent of those whose children had been admitted to hospital care. As the children who had gone into long term hospital care had been more severely disabled than those who remained at home, it appeared that degree of dependency affected the mothers' chances of taking paid employment.

Clear evidence of the effect on parents' employment opportunities of caring for a child with severe disabilities is provided by Bradshaw's (1980) study of Family Fund applicants. Among families applying only 24 per cent contained mothers who were in paid work outside the home, compared to 41 per cent of families in the General Household Survey for a comparable year. In addition, almost a quarter of fathers reported that their employment had been adversely affected by their child's disability.

Another large and representative study of ten-year-old children with a wide range of handicaps and disabilities (Cooke, 1982) showed that parental employment was adversely affected 'in a substantial minority of families [and] that the likelihood of effects on employment increased with the severity of the child's condition' (p87).

Perhaps the most extensive, detailed and methodologically sound study of the economic effects of caring for a disabled child is that of Baldwin (1981 and 1985). This study, which replicated the Family Expenditure Survey for a sample of families with disabled children, showed clearly that the labour market participation of mothers with a severely disabled child was considerably lower (33 per cent) than that of mothers in a control group (59 per cent). In addition, the control group mothers worked longer hours and earned more. These differences increased with the age of the youngest child in the family, indicating that women with disabled children were less likely to rejoin the labour market as their children grew up.

Paid work outside the home is important to women with disabled children for other than purely economic reasons (Burton, 1975; Wilkin, 1979; Glendinning, 1983; Baldwin and Glendinning, 1983). As Glendinning (1983) has documented, the 'overwhelming importance of work outside the home, however menial and lacking in intrinsic job satisfaction [is] the opportunity for a break in a monotonous domestic routine' (p. 74). Indeed, Bradshaw's follow-up study of Family Fund applicants found that mothers who were 'able to do paid work unrestricted' were apparently under less stress than other mothers and that 'mothers who were not able to work but wanted to' were more stressed than mothers who were at home and did not want to do paid work (Bradshaw, 1980). A similar relationship between malaise and the opportunity to work outside the home was revealed in the Child Health and Education Study (Cooke, 1982).

As already suggested, fathers' employment is not immune to the effects of having a disabled or chronically sick child in the family; Burton, Wilkin, Glendinning, Bradshaw and Baldwin have all documented some impact. Baldwin (1985) found that the largest differences in labour market participation between fathers of severely disabled children and fathers of ordinary children occurred among unskilled manual workers, their participation rates being 76.2 per cent and 90.0 per cent respectively.

However, fathers' employment appears not to be as seriously affected as is that of mothers. Fathers tend to miss hours or days at work rather than to give up or lose jobs altogether (Burton, 1975; Wilkin, 1979; Baldwin, 1985). Restrictions on their choice of employment or on promotion opportunities may also occur (Glendinning, 1983; Cooke, 1982; Baldwin, 1985).

Effects of this sort have all been identified in the OPCS survey of children with disabilities (Smyth and Robus, 1989). Nine per cent of mothers of disabled children worked full-time and 31 per cent part-time, compared with 15 per cent and 33 per cent respectively of all mothers. However, as Baldwin's work would predict, this difference was widest among the mothers of children in the oldest age groups, especially in respect of full-time work. Only 16 per cent of mothers with disabled children aged 10-15 years worked full-time, compared with 26 per cent of all mothers. With regard to part-time work, the difference was smaller, 39 per cent compared to 43 per cent.

Fathers' employment was also affected: 73 per cent of those with disabled children were in full-time employment, compared with 88 per cent of all fathers. However, it is not possible to say the extent to which this difference is influenced by socio-economic class.

Fathers of younger children were apparently more severely affected by having a disabled child than were fathers of older children, an effect the reverse of that identified for mothers. Sixty-six per cent of men with disabled children aged 0-4 years were in full-time work, compared with 85 per cent of all fathers with children of this age. In the next age band (5-9 years) the figures were, respectively, 75 per cent and 92 per cent and in the oldest age band (10-15 years) 79 per cent and 89 per cent. Again, however, we do not know how class may affect these distributions nor do we know what cohort effects may be at work. The youngest children in the study were born between 1980 and 1985, a period when younger people particularly suffered from the growth in unemployment. By contrast, the oldest children were born between 1970 and 1975 when their fathers may not have been so vulnerable to job losses. The interplay between class, father's age and having a disabled child remains to be explored from these data.

Parents who were in paid work were asked about the ways in which their employment had been affected by their child's disability. As Table 3.1 shows, mothers were far more likely to identify such effects.

Table 3.1 The ways in which parents felt that their employment had been affected by their child's disability

Ways affected	Men	Women
	% of those in employment mentioning each effect	
Type of work	2	19
Opportunity for changing jobs	7	24
Hours worked	8	31
Promotion prospects	4	15
Distance can travel	4	24
Attendance	13	30
Other	2	1
Total (%)	100	100

Source: Smyth and Robus, 1989, Table 3.1

For both mothers and fathers, however, the most frequently mentioned effects were the number of hours it was possible to work and the need to be away from work from time to time.

Carers of adults with disabilities

Information about the carers of adults who have grown up with disabilities is relatively scarce, although recent studies of young adults give some indication of continuing, and possible increasing, effects on parental employment. For example, some parents of severely disabled young people in one study gave up work when their child left school with no satisfactory weekday occupation (Hirst, 1982). Indeed, the employment patterns of mothers of severely disabled young adults (Hirst, 1984) appear to be very different from those of women in a comparable group in the General Household Survey. They are both less likely to be in paid employment at all and, when they are, less likely to be in full-time jobs. Some 60 per cent of mothers aged under 60 in two-parent families in Hirst's survey were not in paid employment. Of these, 16 per cent had given up employment after their disabled child had turned 16, most often because of the needs of the disabled young person.

The great majority of women who were not in paid employment, regardless of whether they wanted to work or had got used to not working, attributed their lack of paid work outside the home to the limitations brought about by caring for a disabled person. *All* mentioned their son's or daughter's need for personal attention or supervision as a major limitation.

Half of the women who were in employment in Hirst's (1984) survey had experienced some change in their work pattern, related to their daughter's or son's disablement, since the young person had reached 16 years. The most often mentioned effects were times of the day worked and reductions in earnings.

Given the relative paucity of independent living arrangements for adults with disabilities, and a commitment to the reduction of long-term institutional care, it seems that caring for a child with disabilities may become, for some parents, a life-long task with a life-long impact on labour market participation and on living standards.

Caring for adults who acquire disabilities during adulthood might be expected to have a very different impact on employment patterns from that of caring for an adult who has always been disabled, not least because parents are more likely to care for the latter and spouses for the former. Instead of the gradual reduction in mothers' expectations of paid employment outside the home as their disabled children grow to be disabled adults, in households where a member becomes disabled *as an adult*, carers may experience a sudden change in circumstances which makes it impossible for them to continue working. Our knowledge about this aspect of the effect of caring is scanty. Sainsbury (1970), in her study of adult disability, refers only in passing to the fact that the care of a disabled person was 'usually undertaken by one relative within the household [only] who in many cases went out to work as well' (p. 130).

Husbands and wives who take the major responsibility for spouses who are dying, appear to be more likely to experience changes in their employment patterns in the 12 months before their spouse's death than any other group of main carers (Cartwright, 1973). Very few working spouses reported *no* changes in their paid work but wives were more likely to have been affected. In addition, wives caring for their husbands were more likely to have given up work altogether than were husbands caring for their wives; men seemed to cope by taking time off work.

More light has been thrown on this issue recently by the OPCS disability surveys (Martin and White, 1988), although the impact of having a disabled partner on the spouse's labour market participation was not the primary focus of the investigation. In 1985, when the survey was carried out, 78 per cent of all men under pensionable age, and 58 per cent and 62 per cent, respectively, of married and non-married women under pensionable age, were in paid work. By contrast, only 23 per cent of the wives of non-elderly disabled men without dependent children, and 44 per cent of those with, were in paid employment. When it was a non-elderly wife who was disabled, 35 per cent of men without dependent children, and 56 per cent of those with, were in paid work (Table 2.16, Martin and White, 1988). Although there were age effects at work among the couples without dependent children (they were older and the incidence of paid work for both men and women decreases with age), it was clear that even among the younger couples with dependent children, where the need for one or both partners to be earning would be greatest, having a disabled spouse depressed the likelihood of the carer being in paid work.

Further, the survey suggests that the level of male spouse carers' employment was rather more depressed than was that of the female carers. Relative to what might be expected in the general population, male carers' participation was 28 per cent lower when they had dependent children and 55 per cent lower when they did not. By contrast, female spouse carers' rates of labour market participation were reduced, respectively, by 22 per cent and 48 per cent (all figures recalculated from pp. 12-14, Martin and White, 1988).

Without more direct manipulation of the OPCS survey data it is difficult to know how significant this difference is. However, it does have echoes in a recent, in-depth study of 22 non-elderly couples where one partner had a disability or chronic illness, acquired since marriage (Parker, 1989 a and b). This study suggested that, because of their lack of access to part-time work, male spouse carers were more likely than females to experience a 'threshold' effect on their paid work. That is, beyond a certain level of dependency in their wives, men were unable to maintain their full-time paid employment and were unlikely to obtain part-time employment. By contrast, women spouse carers were able to combine paid work and caring because of their access to part-time work. Although tentative, this model might help to explain the OPCS survey findings. It also alerts us to the importance of considering the carers' level of participation in the labour market at the onset of the cared-for persons' need for care and the level of care required, along with the gender of the carer and the alternative employment options available.

Of course, whether or not caring has an impact on the employment of those looking after adults with disabilities will also depend on other factors, such as the provision of services and the nature of the job the carer has. Blaxter (1976), for example, has shown that professionals involved in the care of people with disabilities may make the impact of caring on employment more severe than it need be. Health and social service professionals were not likely to recognise a young disabled woman's need for help with personal care and domiciliary support with the consequence that husbands had to take time off work. However, '[h]ow drastic a step this might be would depend, of course, on the nature of that work: in some cases leave might be granted without trouble but in more, the result was at least financial hardship and at worst the loss of the job. This applied equally, of course, to working wives ... (p. 60).

Thus what we know about the effect of caring for an adult who becomes disabled, gleaned from the studies mentioned above and from more subjective accounts (eg Oliver, 1983; EOC, 1981), suggests that the impact on employment is quite drastic, not least because of its suddenness.

Earnings Obviously lost work opportunities, through loss of a job, not taking up employment as children grow, inability to pursue promotion opportunities and so on all have an economic impact on informal carers. It is only recently, however, that any attempt has been made to put figures to these effects.

Information on this topic comes from three different types of approach. First, there is the analysis of general population surveys which attempts to isolate the earnings effect of providing care of different types (Joshi, 1987). Secondly, there is the very recent report on the financial circumstances of disabled adults living in private households (Martin and White, 1988) which, although not primarily concerned with carers, does shed some light on their circumstances. Finally, there is the research designed specifically to examine the financial impact of caring on particular groups of carers (Hyman, 1977; Nissel and Bonnerjea, 1983; Baldwin et al., 1983; Baldwin 1985; Glendinning, 1989). Each of these approaches is considered below.

Joshi (1987) has reanalysed data from the Women and Employment Survey (Martin and Roberts, 1984) and from the Medical Research Council's Survey of Health and Development (1946 cohort) to examine how caring — for children, husbands, or relatives with disabilities — affects women's labour market participation, their hours of paid work and their pay. She established, first, the very important (although perhaps not surprising) connection between women's need for money and the likelihood of their being in paid employment: 'at any given stage of the family life-cycle and level of alternative resources, the women who are most likely to be in employment are those who would find it most financially rewarding. Similarly, all else being equal, women with the greatest need for cash are more likely to be employed (particularly in part-time jobs) than women who have other resources to fall back on' (p. 115). This conclusion underlines the employment effects identified by Lewis and Meredith and Ungerson (see above).

With regard to loss of earnings, Joshi found that women, giving up work to care for disabled relatives during later stages of the life cycle, would forgo around £8,500 p.a. if childless and around £7,000 p.a. if they had ever had children. (The difference is due to the generally depressive effects of child-bearing on women's life-time earnings). Further, if women are ever able to return to work after caring, their 'subsequent pay might be reduced through loss of seniority' (p. 129) although such effects are probably most serious when women give up paid work early in the life-cycle.

The OPCS disability survey has generated a substantial amount of information about the financial circumstances of people with disabilities from which it is sometimes possible to say something about carers' earnings. For example, the survey shows how important is the presence of a non-disabled spouse who can work; married disabled adults had the highest amounts of earned income amongst all disabled adults 'mainly because there were more earners in the family unit, but also because when only one person was earning it was more likely to be the non-disabled partner with higher average earnings' (p. 19). However, when real incomes were converted into equivalent incomes, in order to compare households of different compositions, it was clear that, relative to other households containing disabled adults, married couples with children had very low incomes, second only to lone parents. Further, when the number of earners in the household was taken into account, married couples with children were shown to be the poorest regardless of whether there was no, one or two earners. When the data were analysed by equivalent net income deciles for the general population (Table 3.24), married couples with children were again shown to be disadvantaged relative to all other groups except lone parents. Thus, even when spouse carers are earning, they do not earn sufficient to redress the impact of their partner's reduced or non-existent earnings.

Children

The OPCS survey of children with disabilities showed that parents' likelihood of being in paid work at all was, apparently, affected by their having a disabled child (see above). The survey also demonstrated effects on parents' earning when they were able to do paid work (Smyth and Robus, 1989). Average gross earnings for people with children for the year in which the disability survey was carried out were 9 per cent higher for men and 7 per cent higher for women in part-time employment than those found among parents of disabled children. The few mothers of disabled children who worked full-time actually had slightly higher earnings than all mothers in full-time paid work. The lower levels of earnings appeared to be accounted for, at least in part, by the disabled children's parents receiving lower hourly rates of pay.

A comparison of average incomes (including benefit payments) in different types of households and with the general population of those with dependent children showed some very interesting patterns. Using equivalent incomes, which control for housing costs and household composition, Smyth and Robus (1989) showed that all types of family containing a disabled child were disadvantaged relative to similar families, except for lone parents (Table 3.2).

Table 3.2 Average net weekly equivalent incomes for different types of families with a disabled child and similar families in the general population

Type of family	Average weekly equivalent income	
	Families with disabled children £	General population with dependent children £
Lone parent	79.01	78.12
Married, one child	115.76	126.20
Married, more than one child	89.79	107.45
Total	91.14	110.25

Source: Smyth and Robus, 1989, Table 3.17

The apparent lack of effect on lone parents' family income is explained by the high proportion of lone parents in both the OPCS survey and in the Family Expenditure Survey (which was used to provide the comparative figures) who were dependent upon benefit income. Families which contain other dependent children as well as the disabled child appeared to be particularly disadvantaged.

As was the case with exploring the impact of having a disabled child on employment prospects, it is not possible from the OPCS survey data to examine inter-relationships between class, age of parents, and having a disabled child and their impact on earnings and income. The third source of information on the impact of caring on carer's incomes is those few studies carried out specifically to examine these effects, plus evidence gleaned from other research on carers which has covered the issue.

Nissel and Bonnerjea (1982), in their pilot study of the costs of caring, estimated the opportunity costs of constraints on the employment of married women caring for an elderly dependent relative at home. Although women who were still managing to work full-time were relatively well paid, those who had part-time jobs were 'in jobs paying well below the average compared with the type of jobs which they previously held' (p. 55). It was clear that women in part-time employment had taken up 'menial jobs in secondary labour markets at hours and in places designed to fit in with their home commitments'. In total, the opportunity costs to families in earnings forgone by wives not in employment, but who would have liked to take up paid work again, was estimated at £87 per week or £4,500 per annum. The opportunity costs of earnings forgone by wives who were in less than full-time employment was £37.00 per week or £1,900 per annum (all at 1982 prices).

A comparison of the earnings of mothers with and without disabled children (Baldwin et al., 1983; Baldwin, 1985) found that employed women with a disabled child earned an average of £7.20 a week less than employed women in a control group. This difference in earnings increased as the age of the youngest child in the family increased. By the time the youngest child was 11 years old, the average weekly earnings of employed women in the control group were £16.30 higher than those of the employed women with disabled children (all 1978 prices). Although Baldwin's evidence of the effect on men's earnings was less conclusive, it suggested, nevertheless, some impact, especially on non-manual workers who earned on average £18.00 a week less than their control counterparts. However, the effect was not uniform across individual occupation groups, being largest (£41.10 per week) among administrative and managerial workers but reversed among clerical workers. In this latter group the men with disabled children earned an average of £7.00 a week *more* than their control counterparts. This difference was thought likely to reflect lost promotion opportunities: 'It seems likely that some of these higher earning clerical workers may have missed promotion to administrative and managerial positions because of the child's disablement, remaining at the top of their own salary grades' (Baldwin et al., 1983). Interviews with the fathers of disabled children lent some support to this 'lost promotion' hypothesis. There was thus little evidence in Baldwin's research to suggest that men with a disabled child increased their earnings to compensate for lower earnings by women.

Disability benefits for children, although not designed as income replacement, are almost inevitably used as such. Yet in this study benefits 'evened out earning losses for only one group of families — manual workers with a child under five. They had little impact on the earnings losses of non-manual workers with a disabled child and families with older children' (*ibid*).

Life-cycle effects on total family income were also different between those with disabled children and the controls: 'For both non-manual and manual control families the lower quartile, median and upper quartile of gross incomes rise with the age of the youngest child. This pattern is not exhibited by families with a disabled child' (ibid).

Studies of childhood cancer (Bodkin et al., 1982) and childhood leukaemia (Pentol, 1983), although based on rather small samples, have also documented lost family income, especially during periods of in-patient treatment.

Hyman (cited by EOC, 1982) in her study of the extra costs of disablement, calculated that carers who had had to give up their own employment to care for adults with disabilities had an average loss of earnings of around £120 per week (at 1980 prices). More recently Glendinning (1989) found that, in a sample of 30 carers (caring for someone other than a spouse), only six had experienced no effects on their paid employment and, thereby, their earnings. Although these effects are not quantified they must have been substantial, particularly for the eight who had given up paid work completely.

Given even this small number of studies, it is evident that those caring for dependent relatives experience adverse financial effects. These include not only not being able to take up, or having to give up, paid employment but also, when in work, earning lower amounts than similar people without disabled dependants.

Expenditure

Loss of earnings is only one aspect of the financial cost to the family of caring for a dependent relative. The day-to-day living expenses of a disabled person may be higher than those of another person and the family may have to 'buy in' various services to help care for him or her. As with income, the detailed accounting of these costs is a relatively new development in research. This is not surprising given the complications of the dependent's own financial status and the cash transfers that may take place between household members, to be recouped eventually, perhaps, through legacies after the dependent relative's death. The most detailed work on the extra expenditure incurred by families with a disabled member has concentrated on children (Baldwin, 1977, 1981, 1985; Bodkin et al., 1982; Townsend et al., 1981) where these complications are less in evidence. However, even in these relatively uncomplicated households, the task of accounting for extra expenditure is difficult, as Baldwin's detailed and painstaking unravelling testifies.

Baldwin's (1977) study, based on subjective estimates by parents themselves, indicated that 90 per cent of a sample of families with a disabled child had extra costs associated with the disability. The average amount over and above normal child care costs spent in a year was estimated at £118.92 (equivalent to around £245 at 1980 prices, calculated by EOC, 1982), although there was a wide range. Nearly all families spent money on extra clothes and bedding and over half had costs associated with incontinence equipment. Extra washing and heating, transport costs, special food and diets, housing and house adaptations, repairs to house and furniture, aids to mobility and daily living all caused extra expenditure in at least some of the households studied.

Baldwin's later (1981 and 1985) study used a different approach, comparing the income and expenditure patterns of a sample of families with severely disabled children with those of a control group of families with children drawn from the Family Expenditure Survey. To a great extent this study substantiated the findings of research based on parents' own accounts.

It was found that families with disabled children incurred extra expense on items bought regularly, such as food, fuel, transport and children's clothing. The level of extra expense varied with family income and the way extra expense was defined. However, for families with incomes between £70 and £100 a week it was estimated that nothing less than an extra £15 a week (at 1984 prices) would have a significant impact on these everyday costs. In addition extra expense was caused at intervals by larger costs, such as house adaptations, and hospitalisation.

The OPCS survey of children with disabilities has identified a number of items on which their families spend extra money because of the disability (Smyth and Robus, 1989). For example, over a third of families had, at some stage, acquired at least one item of special equipment or had some adaptation made to their car or home. However, only 13 per cent had done so (and paid themselves) and in the 12 months before the survey. Average expenditure on such items was £234. Apart from additional expenditure on toiletries bought from a chemist, over two-thirds (68 per cent) of families had spent money regularly on items or services required solely because of the child's disability. The average amount spent was £1.72 per week but this varied substantially. Over a third (36 per cent) said that they spent an average of £1.13 a week extra on chemist's items because of the child's disability. Finally, 70 per cent were able to point to additional expenditure on 'normal' items and services such as clothing, fuel and food. The average additional expenditure here was £7.65 per week.

Averaged among all families with a disabled child total additional weekly expenditure was £6.54 but this varied by severity. Families whose children were the most severely disabled (severity categories 9-10) were spending £12.53 compared with the £4.55 being spent by families with the least disabled children.

As Baldwin found, the extra amount spent varied with income, those on the highest incomes spending the most. 'Families with the lowest incomes (£0-80) and very severely disabled children (severity category 9-10) were spending an average £6.49 per week, less than half the amount [£15.47] spent by those families with the highest incomes (over £170) whose children were similarly disabled ...' (Smyth and Robus, 1989, p. 40). Not surprisingly, those on the lowest equivalent incomes were the most likely to say that they needed to spend more on their disabled child's needs but were unable to do so. Nearly half (46 per cent) of those with an equivalent income of £60 a week or less 'needed something for their child which they could not afford to buy' (Smyth and Robus, 1989, p. 40).

As has already been suggested, untangling the extra costs of caring for a disabled adult is, if anything, even more complicated and such detailed work as Baldwin's has not been undertaken on a sample of adults. However, Hyman's study of adults confined to wheelchairs estimated average extra expenditure of £1,803 per year (1980 prices calculated by the EOC, 1982), and the OPCS disability survey has identified at least some of the extra costs of disablement (Martin and White, 1988). In the survey of disabled adults lump sum purchases, related to the disability, made in the previous 12 months were identified, as was regular expenditure on items required solely because of the disability, and on items required by most people but on which disabled people may spend more. Only 16 per cent of disabled adults had made lump sum purchases in the previous year but the majority had the two types of regular expenditure (60 per cent and 71 per cent respectively). Taken together the average additional regular expenditure was £6.10 per week, ranging from an average of £3.20 for the least severely disabled up to an average of £11.70 for the most severely disabled. However, there was very wide variation, particularly with income. For example, additional expenditure for the most severely disabled people with disposable incomes of under £40 per week was £8.20, compared to £23.40 a week for those with disposable incomes of £120 per week or more.

This is an effect also described by Baldwin and Hyman, suggesting that low income families containing disabled individuals have the double disadvantage of extra needs but few resources to meet them.

Clearly these figures are substantially lower than those indicated by Baldwin or Hyman, particularly when the intervening period of price inflation is taken into account. There are a number of reasons why this may be. First, as already stated, the survey was not, indeed could not be, as comprehensive as Baldwin's and, further, did not use a control group. Secondly, the approach used required respondents to identify extra costs rather than, as in Baldwin's study, asking them to fill in a diary. As Martin and White acknowledge, it was often difficult for respondents to estimate additional expenditure on 'normal' items and services such as food and heating. Further, the questions were directed to the person with the disability rather than, necessarily, the person responsible for household expenditure. Thirdly, both Baldwin and Hyman used samples of severely disabled individuals and, therefore, identified costs at the top end of the range. Fourthly, the figures presented are averaged across all disabled adults, not just across those who were able to identify any additional expenditure.

While Martin and White's figures do, perhaps, need to be interpreted with a little caution they do, for the first time, give us an idea of the minimum extra costs incurred by disabled adults and, by implication, by their carers.

Further, all these studies indicate that, regardless of the amounts involved, any extra expenditure on the person with the disability means that expenditure on the carers' needs is reduced, particularly when total household income is low.

The Physical Costs of Caring

The 'daily grind' of caring for a dependent relative, whether a child, an adult or an elderly person, has now been well documented (Bayley, 1973; Wilkin, 1979; Glendinning, 1983 and 1985; Levin et al., 1983; Ayer and Alazewski, 1984; Parker, 1989). Lifting up and down stairs, in and out of bed, bath and wheelchair; doing extra housework or housework made more difficult by the presence of a dependent relative; special cooking; feeding a helpless person; coping with incontinence and the extra bed making and washing it causes; the difficulties of getting out of the house to do essential shopping: these are just some of the difficulties with which carers must cope. However, while it is undoubtedly the case that many informal carers are not in good health themselves, it is not at all clear that poor *physical* health and caring are causally linked.

For example, while only a third of the informal carers of elderly mentally infirm people in one study rated their own health as good, and about half had disabilities which limited their activities (Levin et al., 1983), their average age was 61 years. As the General Household Survey regularly shows, around two-thirds of people over the age of 45 report chronic health problems. Similarly, almost half of the carers in another study of dependent elderly people (Charlesworth et al., 1983) reported that their health was less than good but, again, the majority of carers were themselves 50 years of age or older. Indeed, only 9 per cent of the total sample felt that their ill health had been directly caused by their caring responsibilities, and 13 per cent that caring had probably worsened already poor health.

The problem of causality in relation to poor health is no less equivocal among parents of children with disabilities. While, as Philp and Duckworth (1982) have reported, many studies 'suggest a high prevalence or incidence of problems' with health among parents, the only study to have employed a control group (Gath, 1977 cited by Philp and Duckworth) 'suggests that long-term health problems do not occur among mothers caring for a child with disablement any more than they do among mothers generally' (p. 33). Moreover, no study appears ever to have controlled adequately for the intervening variable of social class.

Arguing about whether or not the physical burdens of caring cause physical health problems is, perhaps, a *canard*. Carers undoubtedly do experience a level of physical exertion in their daily living, far above that experienced by other people, which restricts their lives in many ways. Moreover, physical ill-health does appear to be associated with reduced duration of informal care (Levin et al., 1983). The question to be answered is: what is the best way of relieving this physical burden to allow carers to lead more normal lives? To do this, however, far more detailed information is needed about what carers actually *do*, and how much of their time is taken up with caring tasks. A start in this direction was made by Nissel and Bonnerjea's pilot study, employing time budgets to measure both the amount of time main carers spent on caring tasks and the amount of help they received from others. This type of work needs to be extended to other dependency groups and carers (Nissel, 1984).

The Emotional Costs of Caring

While the burdens of caring do not appear to have an easily defined effect on physical health, many researchers have produced evidence that they bring about increased levels of stress or emotional strain (eg Isaacs et al., 1972; Cartwright, 1973; Tew and Laurence, 1975; Bradshaw and Lawton, 1978; Gledhill et al, 1982; Cook, 1982; Levin et al., 1983; Gilleard et al., 1984; Quine and Pahl, 1985; Clarkson et al., 1986).

To talk about the 'stress' experienced by those caring for dependent relatives is, however, to beg many questions. Although the suggestion that carers may suffer from stress has an immediate intuitive appeal, its assessment or measurement is fraught with difficulties.

First, the experience of stress can vary both inter- and intra-personally. Two people experiencing the same 'stressful' situation may feel themselves to be under quite different degrees of stress. Even one individual may feel differently about the same situation at different points in his or her life.

Secondly, 'objective' measures of stress, eg the Malaise Inventory (Rutter et al., 1970), the General Health Questionnaire (Goldberg, 1972), rest on the assumption that physical or psychological symptoms are phenomena parallel to, or concomitant with, the experience of stress. As recent work has suggested (Hirst, 1983; Hirst and Bradshaw, 1983), this may not necessarily be so.

Thirdly, the experience of stress may be socially or culturally mediated to some extent. Society's expectations about what carers should or should not be expected to do for those they care for may vary across time, between classes or genders, or between generations, affecting perceptions of what is, and what is not, stressful. For example, Ungerson, in her writing on women and caring (Ungerson, 1983) has identified caring tasks which in Western European society are designated 'female' and those which are designated 'male'. Not everyone would agree with Ungerson's explanation of these differences in terms of taboo. However, evidence about service providers' readiness to establish domiciliary support or provide residential care when 'normal' gender boundaries are crossed (see Chapter 4) suggests that they may see certain tasks as less suitable (and perhaps, therefore, more stressful) for men to carry out than for women. If service providers differentiate in this way there seems every possibility that carers will do so themselves.

The assessment of stress in carers is, then, not unequivocal. In the context of this review, however, it is reasonable to suggest that it is carers' subjective perceptions of stress which are the most important. That a carer feels that she can no longer 'carry on' is of more concern here than the fact that her neighbour may be coping with a similar burden under similar circumstances.

It might be asked whether it actually 'matters' that informal carers experience higher levels of stress than do other members of the population. If we are concerned with questions of equity it certainly matters if some people experience more stress than others because of the responsibility they take on for dependent members of the population. On a more pragmatic level, it matters that carers experience high levels of stress if this means that their ability to continue caring is reduced.

Evidence from studies of those caring for elderly mentally infirm people certainly suggests that stress influences outcome in terms of the duration of informal care. Levin et al. (1983) found that the level of carers' strain, measured by the General Health Questionnaire at an initial interview, was strongly associated with outcome 12 months later. Where carers had been experiencing a high level of strain, the surviving elderly people were more likely to have been placed in permanent institutional care, even when the carers had wanted to go on caring. 'Despite their willingness to care, [they] were generally worn down by the strain which caring imposed' (p. 235). Moreover, the mental health of those who had continued to care had declined, while that of those whose relatives had died or entered long-term care had improved.

Similarly, Gilleard, et al. (1981) showed that in a group of elderly mentally ill people, the presence of 'demand' problems (see p. 84) which were associated with high levels of stress in carers, were the only factors predictive of outcome. Carers reporting fewer than the median number of 'demand' problems were more likely to continue caring for their dependent relative in the community than were those reporting a higher than median number.

Although recent evidence on admission to long-term care for children with disabilities is limited, there is some suggestion that the main carer's emotional state may influence outcome. Wilkin (1979) reports that more mothers whose mentally handicapped children were awaiting admission to care, reported problems with their mental health, and were more likely to have received treatment for them, than did those whose children were to remain at home.

Although there may be important intervening variables at play between stress and admission to care (eg the reactions of professionals who are 'gatekeepers' to long-term care facilities) it seems likely that high levels of stress over a long period will affect the duration of informal caring arrangements.

If stress does contribute to breakdown in caring then a reduction in stress levels may prolong it. However, successful intervention requires that we know which aspects of the burden of caring are most taxing and which, if any, of these burdens *can* be reduced and how.

The remainder of this sub-section considers some of the evidence on what creates, and influences levels of, stress for informal carers and then examines what factors appear to alleviate or reduce stress.

The Mediation of Stress

Evidence about the correlates of stress in carers is equivocal, although there is a suggestion in the research literature that what causes stress in the carers of elderly mentally infirm people is not the same as that which causes stress in the carers of non-elderly adults, or in the carers of children with disabilities.

Among carers of elderly people, some studies have indicated that both the age and the level of dependency of the cared-for person (Sheldon, 1948; Isaacs et al., 1972) and the age of the carer (Isaacs et al.) may influence the carers' experience of stress. However, work by Levin et al. (1983) has failed to find any association between the age of elderly confused people, or age of their carers, and stress as measured by the General Health Questionnaire, while Gilleard et al., 1984 suggest that older carers experience *less* strain than younger ones.

Similarly, sex of the main carer and dependent person and the kin relationship between them appear to be related to measured levels of stress in some studies but not in others. Gilhooly's study of those caring for patients with senile dementia (1983 and 1984) found that the *only* characteristic of the dependent person significantly correlated with the carer's morale was sex. Those caring for a female had better morale and better mental health than those caring for males, a finding replicated by

Gilleard et al., 1984. The carer's sex can be important too, male carers having higher morale (Gilhooly, 1984; Levin et al., 1983).

The distance, in kinship terms, from the cared-for person has also been identified as important in some studies; the more distant the relationship the better being the carer's mental health (Gilhooly, 1984). However, this effect was not identified in Levin at al's study and in work by Jones and Vetter (1984) carers who were daughters were found to be more stressed than those who were wives.

Much of this confusion appears to arise because there has been little attempt at multi-variate analysis and no attempt to tie in quantitative analysis with knowledge derived from qualitative work on caring. Thus, the inter-relationships between age and sex of the carer, sex and level of dependency of the cared-for person, and the kin relationship between them are rarely considered, when qualitative research has suggested that, in combination, these variables are likely to be very important in the mediation of stress. For example, Gilleard et al. (1984) talk about the different levels of strain in older and younger carers without controlling for the difference in relationship to the cared-for person implied by the differences in age (ie younger carers were mostly daughters, older carers mostly spouses). Similarly, Jones and Vetter (1984) say that carer daughters were more stressed than carer spouses but, apparently, make no attempt to control for co-residence or the dependency of the elderly person. As these variables will clearly co-vary, and may co-vary with stress as well, it is difficult to be confident about the conclusions. However, as we shall see below, it may be that attempting to identify socio-demographic factors which influence carers' experience of stress is, in itself, a chimerical exercise.

Although Gilhooly was unable to identify any aspect of elderly mentally infirm persons' behaviour or personality which influenced stress levels in their carers, this has not been the case with other research. (Part of the reason for the difference between Gilhooly's and others' work may lie in the relative homogeneity of her group and the small sample size. Both factors would reduce the probability of finding significant association.) Isaacs et al. identified the personality of the elderly person, distortions of both personality and behaviour caused by the mental illness and, to a lesser extent, the physical burden of caring as factors which made caring for the elderly person 'overwhelming'. More statistically sophisticated work carried out in Scotland (Gilleard et al., 1981) studied the inter-relationships between the mood states of those caring for elderly mentally infirm people and problems experienced in caring for them. Five dimensions or factors were identified among the problems of caring: dependency, disturbance, disability, demand and wandering. The 'demand' factor (the attentional and emotional demands that the elderly infirm people made on their carers, for example disrupting the carer's personal social life, always asking questions, demanding attention, creating personality clashes) contributed most to reported levels of strain. Once this source of stress was taken into account none of the other problem factors made any significant contribution to perceived stress.

Levin et al. also identified several factors which contributed to stress among carers of confused elderly people. Heavy incontinence, trying behaviour, night disturbance, and the inability to converse normally were all factors in the cared-for person associated with carers' high stress scores on the General Health Questionnaire. Restrictions on the carers' own leisure activities and the time that could be spent with friends and families — problems associated with 'demand' in Gilleard's work — were also important.

There is much less research on stress among carers of non-elderly adults with disabilities and what there is tends to come from the medical literature. Consequently carers' stress is often seen as an adjunct to the 'patients' well-being or recovery, rather than as a phenomenon (and a concern) worthy of consideration in its own right.

Some of the effects identified in this literature are specific to the type of disability sustained by the cared-for person while others appear to be more general. For example, some studies suggest that carers who are the wives of disabled men experience higher stress levels than do mothers who are carers, especially when the disability is associated with changed behaviour or personality (Thomsen, 1974; Rosenbaum and Najenson, 1976). Similarly, Lovelock (1981a) found that relationship to the cared-for person was an important mediating variable. In his study of a care attendant scheme over two-thirds of wives who were carers appeared to be under severe strain compared with only a third of husbands and half of the parents of disabled children. Unfortunately, Lovelock does not discuss *why* wives might have been more stressed than other carers nor does he attempt any multi-variate analysis.

Regardless of the relationship of carer to cared-for person, particular types of changes associated with disablement appear to be more stress-inducing than others. Changes in personality associated with head injury have been shown to be more stressful than say, any impaired mobility or degree of physical disability that results from the injury (Thomsen, 1974; Oddy et al., 1978). In a related way, aphasia after stroke is associated with higher levels of stress in carers while the severity of physical impairment or overall dependency levels are not (Kinsella and Duffy, 1979).

But again, the picture is not entirely clear. Livingston et al (1985a) found no differences in stress levels between the mothers and wives of head injured men, and Wade et al. (1986) have suggested that carers' stress is more related to the cared-for person's own emotional state than any other factor two years after a stroke.

Evidence about stress levels among those caring for adults who have been disabled since birth or childhood is in even shorter supply.

A study of young adults with severe disabilities (Hirst, 1984), which used the General Health Questionnaire to probe for psychological disturbance in main carers (usually mothers), found no significant relationship between high levels of stress and the nature of the young person's disability or disorder. However, there was a relationship between type of impairment and mothers' stress. Those caring for young adults with only physical impairments had lower recorded stress levels than those caring for young adults with mental or multiple impairments. Although there was no clear relationship between severity of disability overall and the carers' stress levels, there were strongly significant relationships between behaviour disorders and degree of learning difficulties. Taken as a whole, these findings seem to suggest that mothers of young people with disabilities arising from severe intellectual impairment were more likely to suffer stress than were mothers of young people with other disabilities.

Exploration of the relationship between high levels of measured stress in mothers of young disabled children and the variables that might be associated with them has been quite substantial. Here again, however, the results tend to be contradictory.

Bradshaw and Lawton (1978) in one of the earliest British studies of this kind looked at stress levels (using the Malaise Inventory) in the mothers of severely disabled children. They found no relationship between malaise scores and type of disease or impairment, degree of impairment, age of the child and mother, family composition, living standards (measured by social class), standard of housing (measured by basic amenities), or the mother's ability to get out. Those variables which did appear to be related to malaise scores could be classified, although Bradshaw and Lawton did not do so, as:

- **stress ameliorators** – mothers being able to do paid work unrestrictedly when they wanted to; housing which was suitable to the child's needs; satisfaction with the amount of help received in caring for the child; the family being able to take a holiday;

- **stress exacerbators** – night attendance required by the child; the child's inability to play normally (and therefore requiring more attention); the child's poor general health (measured by the need to be a hospital in-patient); the child's hyperactivity; and the parents' health;

- **attitudinal factors** – mothers feeling more restricted though being no less able to get out than other mothers.

(It is interesting to note the high proportion of the stress exacerbators which could be classified under the 'demand' dimension identified by Gilleard et al., 1981.)

Similarly Chetwynd (1985), in a study of mentally handicapped children, found no association between mothers' stress levels and the degree of the child's disability or any specific handicaps the child had. By contrast the child's activity level, the lack of breaks away from the child, and the mothers' perception of a restricted social life were identified as among the most important correlates of stress.

In Quine and Pahl's (1985) study of severely mentally handicapped children, again, diagnostic category was shown not to be related to mothers' stress levels. Similarly, the child's incontinence, lack of mobility, and lack of communication or self-help skills had apparently little effect. When data were combined, however, the *number* of a child's impairments was found to be associated with the mother's stress level. This analysis is particularly convincing because, unlike many other studies, information on the child's disabilities was collected separately (from teachers and care assistants) from information on the mother's stress levels. Quine and Pahl also identified the child's disturbed behaviour, particularly night-time disturbance, and need for a lot of help as being positively associated with maternal stress. A measure of 'adversity' which took into account socio-economic factors such as whether the child was in a two-or one-parent family, the father's occupation, housing conditions, social networks and so on was also important. Multiple regression identified three sets of factors which accounted for a large proportion of the mother's stress levels. Broadly defined these were behavioural problems (including problems related to sleeping); multiple impairments (including problems with the child's health or appearance); and the social and economic circumstances of the family (including the mother's feelings of social isolation, 'adversity' and the presence of money worries).

An opportunity to examine the relationship between carers' stress and child handicap, using a less homogeneous group, was offered by the Child Health and Education Study (Cooke, 1982). Even here 'it was remarkable how few of [the many variables studied] were found to be associated with maternal stress' (p. 52). The presence of incontinence and of impaired intellectual development were related to higher malaise scores in Cooke's research, as they were in that carried out with mothers of spina bifida children by Tew and Laurence (1975). Restricted mobility, by contrast, was not associated with malaise in Cooke's study but was in Tew's and Laurence's. As Bradshaw and Lawton also found, mothers in Cooke's study who were able to take paid work outside the home had lower malaise scores than those who were not. However, the ability to take up paid work outside the home is clearly related to other variables which might influence stress (severity of the child's condition, for example).

To complicate the picture even further, a more recent study of children suffering from spina bifida (Carr et al., 1983) found no significant relationships between the severity or nature of the children's disability, nor between their degree of dependence, and their mother's malaise scores. Such results are in almost total contradiction to those of Tew and Laurence's earlier study of mothers of children with spina bifida.

So far, then, we have considered what aspects of disability and dependence might be responsible for the high levels of stress experienced by informal carers. With the limited exception of carers for elderly mentally infirm people, it has proved difficult to come to any conclusion, however tentative, about this relationship. Carers undoubtedly experience higher levels of stress than the normal population, as measured on the instruments available, yet the intuitively plausible reasons why this might be so (nature and degree of disability, dependence levels, low self-care skills and so on) appear to offer no convincing explanation. Indeed, Bradshaw and Lawton (op. cit.) have gone so far as to suggest that 'the level of stress [experienced by mothers of disabled children] is determined by internal factors — by the physiology and personality of the mother — and that these internal factors are not affected in any specific way by the external social and physical conditions of the family and the child'.

Yet, as was suggested above, Bradshaw and Lawton *did* identify some 'external social and physical' factors which appeared to reduce the mothers' experiences of stress. These were not necessarily related to the child's disability and are difficult to characterise in one word. However, most of these 'stress ameliorators' related to the relief mothers received from the 'daily grind': being able to go out to work, receiving help from other family members, and getting away on holiday.

In other words, this research and some of the other work reviewed here has suggested that there are some aspects of carers' lives that help them to 'cope'. This, as Byrne and Cunningham (1985) have suggested in their comprehensive review of the effects of mentally handicapped children on their families, is an important conceptual distinction. They point to the quantity of research done which aims to discover which families and which family members are most vulnerable to 'the presumed stress of the presence of a mentally handicapped child', yet which has, so far, failed to come to any definite conclusions. This, they conclude, 'suggests that the measurement of gross demographic and structural differences between families provides insufficient information to distinguish between those families who are subject to high levels of stress and those who are not' (p. 859). It seems likely that this is as valid a criticism of the work on stress in other carers as it is of the body of work on those looking after children with disabilities. A more productive approach, Byrne and Cunningham suggest, is one which 'emphasises the fact that many families do cope with and adapt to the stresses they experience and seeks to discover how they do it' (p. 848).

As we have seen already, some of the research which has attempted to explain high levels of carer stress has, willy-nilly, thrown light on what helps mothers, in particular, cope. Is there any indication that similar factors are at work for carers generally?

Getting out of the house

One of the most significant factors in reducing stress levels in carers may be time away from the dependent person, whether as a result of the carer's going out to work or of the cared-for person's being away from home for a time. Levin et al. (1983) found that restrictions on carers' leisure time and on the time they could spend with other people increased the level of stress experienced, while relief care and day care for the dependent relative helped to reduce it. Women in Nissel and Bonnerjea's (1982) study who had given up work to care for an elderly relative, and thus had less opportunity to be away from their dependant, were felt to be starting to accept themselves as 'nobodies', losing perspective on their situation and giving up the right to time of their own. Thompson and Haran's (1985) study of those caring for people who had had a leg amputated also found lower levels of stress among those still in paid work.

Evidence for the relationship between work outside the home and reduced stress levels in the mothers of disabled children and young adults is very strong. Bradshaw and Lawton (1976), Cooke (1982) and Hirst (1984) have all reported lower stress levels among women able to work outside the home. In addition, as already noted above, Bradshaw and Lawton recorded much higher malaise inventory scores among mothers who wanted to work but were not able to than among those who stayed at home but did not want to work outside the home.

More qualitatively oriented work has also shown the value of time away from the cared-for person in relieving the carer's sense of strain.

Help from others

Neither the measurement of help given to main carers by other informal helpers, nor the subsequent analysis of this information, is very sophisticated. It is not surprising, then, to discover that evidence about the relationship between the amount of such help and stress among main carers is equivocal. However, several studies have now shown that satisfaction with, or lack of resentment about, the help given to the main carer by other relatives of the dependent person is associated with reduced stress levels. This effect has been shown among carers of elderly, mentally infirm people (Gilhooly, 1986) as well as among the carers of disabled children (Bradshaw and Lawton, 1978; Glendinning, 1983). There is also a suggestion that a similar effect is evident among carers of frail elderly people who are not necessarily mentally ill as well (Nissel and Bonnerjea, 1982).

Provision of services

Services which are available to informal carers and their dependent relatives will be discussed in more detail in the next section. However, it is worth pointing out here that certain types of services have been identified with lowered stress levels in main carers, albeit in small-scale research projects.

Visits from home helps and community nurses were identified as important in Gilhooly's (1984) and in Levin et al's (1983) studies of those caring for the mentally infirm. By contrast, day care in psycho-geriatric day hospitals does not always appear to reduce stress (Gilhooly, 1984; Gledhill et al., 1982; Smith and Cantley, 1983a and b). This is a finding that seems to run counter to intuition. Gilleard et al., as already noted, identified the emotional and attentional demands which dependent people make on their carers as the most important contributory factors to the experience of stress. So much so that they stated that: '... the key to maintaining community care in the supported elderly mentally infirm ... resides most importantly in the ability of the health services to significantly reduce the strains upon the supporter, by reducing the emotional and attentional demands that are made upon them by their dependents'.

One would expect, then, that day care, by removing the elderly infirm person from the home, would bring some relief to the carer. However, it seems that the nature of some forms of day care may miltiate against this relief. As Smith and Cantley have documented, although care at a psycho-geriatric day hospital may be appreciated by relatives for the relief it brings, it does not 'solve' the problems they are experiencing. Attendance at the day hospital may involve the carer in extra work, getting the dependent person dressed and ready to be picked up at a certain hour. The hours for which the dependent person is absent 'may not coincide with those times at which the patient constitutes the greatest problem for the relatives ...' (p. 34). This finding stands as a cav*eat* to professionals wishing to develop services which they believe would help carers without first discovering what carers themselves would prefer (see Chapter 4).

The impact of residential care, whether short-term or long-term, on carers' stress appears to vary with dependency group. While both short-term hospital care (McKay et al., 1983) and long-term hospital or institutional care (Levin et al.; Challis et al., 1988), have been shown to reduce stress levels dramatically among carers of elderly people, the same is not necessarily true for carers of children with disabilities. Recent evidence has suggested that parents may experience greater stress as a result of their children receiving respite care in hospitals or institutions than if the children had stayed at home. By contrast, respite care with another family may be beneficial (Oswin, 1981). These issues will be covered in more detail in the next section of the review.

In summary, then, the research that has been done demonstrates clearly that people caring for dependent relatives do experience levels of stress higher than those prevalent in the population at large. This seems to be the case regardless of dependency group although less information is available about carers of non-elderly adults and elderly people without mental infirmities than about other carers. What brings about these higher levels of stress is not always clear. Studies which have attempted to identify characteristics of the carer, or cared-for, or of their environment which account for increased stress have often produced confusing, counter-intuitive and contradictory results. Whether this confusion is due to the measures of stress used, the questions asked, the differences in analysis, or whether it reflects real phenomena is unclear. Certainly, it would not be very surprising to discover that the contradictory results were due to real differences between carers of people in different dependency groups. Until a single study examines the experience of stress across different types and ages of carers and dependency groups this confusion will not be resolved.

It may, of course, be the case that research into the stress experienced by carers has approached the question from the wrong angle. Given that people caring for dependent relatives, whether young or old experience more stress than is the norm, and given that the nature and degree of impairment, and to some extent the nature and degree of dependence, are immutable, it might be more sensible to direct future attention to those factors which seem to reduce stress levels. There are already indications that relief from the 'daily grind' of care and help received with it may contribute to such reductions.

Conclusions

For those who take on the role of informal carer for dependent adults and children the costs can be substantial. Carers of the elderly, non-elderly and children alike are often forced to give up work, or lose time if they continue in paid employment, in order to continue caring. Lost or reduced earnings and lost opportunities for promotion have been documented, and increased expenditure in order to care for the dependent person appears to be almost inevitable.

The impact of caring is not solely economic; the 'daily grind' of tasks undertaken while caring for a dependent person is considerable. While any directly causal link between caring and physical ill-health is, as yet, unproven there is clear evidence of the toll imposed on the mental well-being of carers.

It is difficult to draw any firm conclusions about what, if any, characteristics of the carer or cared-for person influence the level of stress carers experience. However, it seems clear that it is possible to reduce the experience of stress. Getting away from the cared-for person for a few hours, being happy with the amount of help received from other members of the family, and receiving domiciliary and day-care services have all been found to be associated to some extent with lowered stress levels.

The research reviewed here has shown that there is an additional dimension to the detailing of the costs of caring — gender — which has only relatively recently received attention. Generally, female carers have been shown to be more likely to give up their jobs, lose more money and to experience more stress than are male carers. Policy makers and service providers alike have yet to acknowledge fully, let alone attempt to remedy, this very significant inequality.

Although we now know substantial amounts about the

costs of care this information is still patchy. For example, the difficulties encountered by those caring for non-elderly adults have received little attention. Similarly, though we know a good deal about the financial impact of caring for heavily dependent children, there is next to no information about this for adults and elderly people. A start has been made but there is clearly a long way to go in this inherently difficult field.

Finally, while there are indications that the provision of services to carers and their dependants might ease, and perhaps prolong, the duration of informal care, we still know relatively little about what type of service might serve what type of carer best. This important issue brings us directly to the subject matter of the next chapter.

Chapter 4

Supporting the Carer

Introduction

If policies are to be developed with the aim of supporting informal care and those who carry it out, and if the best, most cost-effective schemes for such support are to be identified, several questions need to be answered. These are:

- What support is given at present to informal carers by statutory and voluntary health and welfare services and on what criteria are these services allocated?
- What are the objectives, if defined, of providing support? Is the primary aim to maintain dependent people in the community for as long as possible or is the primary aim to relieve the stress experienced by carers?
- How successful are different forms of support in achieving their objectives?
- What services would carers themselves like to receive? What are their needs for support and what do they think would best meet these needs?

Unfortunately the extent to which each of these questions can be answered varies.

First, there have, to date, been relatively few developments within existing service structures which have had the explicit aim of supporting informal carers. Conventional health and welfare services typically see the dependent person, rather than his or her carer, as their client. Any support which accrues to a carer is thus usually a secondary, and often unintentional, result. Consequently, carers' needs, or the way in which they might best be helped, are rarely taken account of in any systematic way. Despite the proliferation of accounts of services intended to support carers, instances of planned and monitored intervention are still comparatively scarce (Twigg, 1989b).

Secondly, as Twigg (1989a) has pointed out, the ways in which carers are perceived by service providers varies, often in not very systematic ways. For example, carers can be seen as part of the structure within and by which dependent people are supported and thus part of the 'taken for granted' resources available to the service provider. Alternatively, the carer can be seen as a co-worker, striving with the service provider towards the aim of keeping the dependent person in the community. Finally, Twigg states, carers can be seen as clients, the legitimate recipients of services aimed at supporting and helping them rather than the dependent person, as such.

The existence of these different models of carers (which can be evident singly or in combination both in the actual practice of any individual service provider and within the service agency) thus makes the stating of objectives *vis a vis* carers difficult. Under one model the objectives may be to keep the carer going as a 'resource' for as long as possible, or to 'improve' her or his practice. In the second model the objective may be to interweave the carer's contribution with the service provider's to provide a 'seamless robe' of support for the dependent person. In some instances this might actually involve stimulating caring inputs from members of the dependent person's networks or beyond, thus involving people who were not previously carers. In the third model the objective may be to reduce the carer's stress or to increase morale, objectives which might, as their logical outcome, involve persuading the carer to give up care.

Thirdly, the lack of clarity of objectives, coupled with the difficulty of applying 'classical' methods of evaluation in this area (Twigg, 1988), make it difficult to see how, or even if, objectives are being achieved.

It is only in relation to the fourth question, what carers' needs are and how they might best be met, that there is any degree of certainty about the answer. The past few years have seen a growth in our knowledge about this topic and, as was indicated in Chapter 3, a growing sophistication in our understanding about what helps to reduce carers' experience of stress. In this chapter the focus is, first, on what is known about carers' own needs and preferences for support. This is followed by an examination of 'conventional' services — such as home help, community nursing, meals-on-wheels — and the ways in which their allocation appears to discriminate against informal carers. Innovative service developments will then be reviewed.

The extent to which services meet service providers' objectives (where articulated) or carers' needs will be addressed only briefly as this area has been reviewed recently by Twigg (1989b).

The Views of Carers

Support for dependent people and their carers can take three principal forms: home-based inputs of domiciliary and nursing (and sometimes medical) care; relief care provided either at home or elsewhere; and cash benefits.

The 1980 and 1985 GHS and the OPCS surveys of disability have told us a lot about the distribution of the first two types of services to dependent people with and without carers (see below). However, it is still the case that there has been no large-scale investigation of the views of *carers,* either about the services that they and those they care for receive or about those they would like to receive. Research information has to be gleaned, for the most part, from studies which did not have the identification of needs or measurement of satisfaction with services as their main aim.

The opinions of those caring for children with disabilities appear to have been canvassed more often than those of people caring for other types of dependants. Overall, conventional service provision — health visiting, social work, respite care — has not appeared to meet parents' needs (eg. Glendinning, 1983; Wilkin, 1979; Ayer & Alaszewski, 1984). Moreover, when parents have been asked about their needs, they have often expressed a desire for services which are not usually provided by statutory bodies. For example, a considerable need for child care during school holidays and at the weekends has been identified among mothers of mentally handicapped children (Wilkin, 1979; Carey, 1982). By contrast, relatively few mothers felt that they needed help with domestic or physical child-care tasks. Wilkin has speculated that:

> ...the high level of felt need in relation to child minding as compared with physical care suggests that mothers regarded it as important to be relieved of the responsibility for tasks rather than only being helped... .To have someone help with changing nappies or dressing the handicapped child may be useful, but to have someone look after the children during the holidays or baby-sit in the evenings actually releases the mother to be able to do something else or just relax without responsibilities. (p.176)

At first sight, Wilkin's suggestion seems somewhat at variance with other studies which have indicated that parents are not always happy about or prepared to use respite care facilities which would give them time away from their child (Glendinning, 1983; Wilkin, 1979; Carey, 1982). However, until recently 'the chief source of relief care has been in hospitals or other institutions, which parents have generally viewed with understandable suspicion and distaste' (Ward, 1982 p.47). Parents who are offered respite care in purpose-built or adapted accommodation, or who are able to use short-term fostering, appear to be much happier with the service (Oswin, 1981; Ayer and Alaszewski, 1984). These newer forms of respite care provision are described below.

Evidence from studies of the elderly also suggests that 'time-off' from the daily grind of caring is valued by carers. Nissel and Bonnerjea's (1982) respondents reported day care as the most appreciated form of help and most would have liked more, although the 'time-off' it provided was never used by the women carers for leisure or pleasure activities. Respite care was also gratefully received although, as will be described below, it is not without its drawbacks. Carers in this study identified one important gap in provision; elderly people, who were too ill for an ordinary local authority home and not ill enough for hospital, had little chance of being offered respite care.

Another small-scale study (Gilhooly, 1986) identified the importance of day care for those caring for elderly, mentally infirm dependants. However, although carers valued the service, the average number of days of care received (two) was felt to be too few to be of substantial benefit. Others have reported that although carers are grateful for the small amount of relief afforded by day care, often this does not offset the amount of time and effort required to get the elderly person ready to go out. Also, the hours at which day care is available are not always those which best meet carers' needs for relief (Emmerson and Fennel, cited in Fennel, 1982; Smith and Cantley, 1983a).

Although the research evidence is relatively scarce, much information about the nature of carers' needs is emerging from the carers' self-help movement (eg. Bonney, 1984 and Pitkeathly, 1989) and from projects which aim to canvas carers' opinions as a preliminary to service development (eg. Birmingham Special Action Project, Jowell and Prior, 1989; London Borough of Croydon, King's Fund Informal Caring Programme, 1988). Taken together these various sources of information suggest a 'core' of main areas of need: information and advice about caring; assessment and review of their needs and those of the person they care for; financial support; training; help in the tasks of caring including respite care; and emotional support (King's Fund Informal Caring Programme, 1988).

Whatever the core areas of need are, however, it is obvious that any individual carer's needs will be determined by her or his personal circumstances — age, sex, household composition, labour market participation, and so on. Thus the form that adequate financial support, for example, might take for an elderly man caring for a frail wife is likely to be different from that for a younger single woman caring for a frail mother or that for a married woman caring for a disabled child. Having identified core needs must not beguile us into thinking that we have also identified the most appropriate form by which to meet those needs.

'Conventional' Services for the Dependent Person and his or her Carer

Conventional forms of support for dependent people (and by implication any informal carers they may have) are, broadly speaking: home help services, meals-on-wheels, community or district nursing, day care and institutional based respite care. There may also be inputs from chiropody services. While we now know a considerable amount about the distribution of these traditional forms of support (particularly in relation to elderly people and their carers), as already suggested, systematic evidence about their usefulness to carers is not available (see Twigg, 1989b).

This dearth of knowledge is to some extent, a reflection of organisational fragmentation (between health and welfare services, between statutory and voluntary provision) which currently makes manipulation of resources to achieve an optimum 'package' of support very difficult (Challis and Davies, 1980). Even so, there has been little research on the importance or effectiveness of these individual forms of support.

This failure to focus explicitly on carers and to assess the extent and effectiveness of different types of support within a single research project inevitably means that the evidence reported here will be fragmentary. We begin, nevertheless, by reviewing evidence about what services are provided by whom and attempting to discover the criteria used in allocating them.

Domiciliary and day care services

In general, the evidence is that domiciliary services supplied to dependent people, which might also help their carers, are insufficient. More importantly, in this context, they appear often to be allocated by criteria which discriminate against informal carers. There is now a substantial body of evidence which shows that the bulk of certain types of service provision exists to support dependent people who live alone rather than those who live with others. The 1985 GHS, for example, shows that the main dependants of carers who lived elsewhere were twice as likely to receive regular visits from their GP or a social worker, four times as likely to have a home help and ten times as likely to receive meals-on-wheels as were those whose carers were in the same household (Green, 1988). Much of this effect seems likely to be accounted for by the high proportion of dependants with a carer in a different household who lived by themselves. There was, however, little difference in levels of contact with community or district nurses.

Surveys of adults with disabilities show that support from statutory services is at a low level and appears to be even lower when other family members are available to care; for example, Harris's survey (Harris, 1971) suggested that living with others affected not only whether services were received at all but also influenced the provision of particular services. Where there was a demonstrable need (severe disability) which could not obviously be met by carers (eg. for nursing care) there was little difference in provision between those living alone and those living with others. By contrast, the home help service was six times more likely, and meals on wheels eight times more likely, to be provided to those living alone. Occupying an intermediate position, chiropody was only twice as likely to be provided to people with severe disabilities who were living alone.

The recent OPCS disability surveys show similar patterns. Among the most severely disabled adults (severity categories 9 and 10), those who were single and living alone were three times as likely as those who were married and seven times as likely as those who were single and living with others to have a local authority home help. In the next severity category down (7–8) it was those dependent people who were married who were least likely to get a home help (11 per cent compared with 15 per cent of those who were single and living with others and 61 per cent of those who were single and living alone). The provision of meals-on-wheels varied in a similar way (Martin, White and Meltzer, 1989 table 4.21). Contact with 'professional' service providers, such as social workers, community nurses, or general practitioners, by contrast, did not seem to vary with the household circumstances of the disabled person in this survey.

This evidence suggests some form of 'hierarchy' in service providers' minds about the responsibility of carers to carry out certain tasks; carers in the same household being apparently less likely to be expected to attend to the nursing care of dependent people than to cook their meals or do their housework.

This issue of the 'substitutability' of services, i.e. the extent to which informal carers *can* substitute for formal services, is one developed in Arber's work on the GHS. She confirms that domestic services are essentially substitutable by any available carer, while personal health and hygiene services are only partially substitutable, depending on the relationship between the carer and the cared-for person. For example, elderly married couples in the 1980 GHS appeared to perform for one another 'at least some of the functions otherwise carried out by a district nurse' (Arber et al, 1988, p.169), while a relationship between the generations *and* across the sexes, made a large difference to receipt of services of this sort. District nursing support was thus twice as likely to be provided 'where the unmarried adult carer [was] caring for an elderly person of the opposite sex' (p.169) as where it was a person of the same sex being cared for.

As this work suggests, it is not just whether or not the elderly person lives alone that determines service receipt but also, if not living alone, the composition of the rest of the household.

This was evident in Harris's (1971) survey, where receipt of services was related both to household size and to the nature of the relationship between carer and cared-for person. Very severely handicapped people living with their spouse *and* married children were less likely to receive services than those living with married children alone. Similarly, those living with married children only were less likely to receive services than those living with an unmarried child (whom one might expect to be the only family member left at home). This reduction in the receipt of services with reduction in the number of people in the household did not, however, obtain for those living entirely alone or only with a spouse. This suggests that domiciliary service provision was sometimes used to prevent carers giving up employment. The fewer other people there were in a household who might provide financial support, the *more* likely were services to be received, thus enabling the carers' continued paid employment outside the home.

Other, smaller scale, studies of elderly people (Allen, 1983), of disablement in adults (Sainsbury, 1970), and of carers (Bristow, 1981; Charlesworth et al, 1983) reveal similar patterns of provision:

> Persons who lived alone depended predominantly upon local authority welfare services. Those living in two-person households depended mainly on relatives for help, but received a considerable amount of help from welfare services as well. Few persons in other types of household received help from welfare services ... local authority services were substitutes for family help. Domiciliary services were not sufficiently developed to play a well-defined supporting role where disabled persons lived with their families. (Sainsbury, 1970, p.145-46)

The role of statutory authorities in supporting carers who are also breadwinners appears to emerge from Arber's work also (Arber et al, 1988):

> The bulk of both male and female unmarried adults who live with a sole elderly person are in full-time paid employment *and* will be seen by service providers as the prime breadwinner for the household. Over half the married women [carers] were in paid employment, although the majority, 57 per cent, worked part-time. Service providers may see work as less central for married women, because they will generally not be the prime breadwinner and therefore less in need of support. (p.168 original emphasis)

A further variable (implicit in some of what has gone before) which appears to influence domiciliary service provision to those looking after dependent people is the sex of the carer. We have seen that women undertake the bulk of informal care, yet gender has been identified as an important issue only recently (Land, 1978; Finch and Groves, 1980 and 1983; Finch, 1984; Dalley, 1988); indeed, early research on dependency rarely differentiated between male and female carers. More recent research, however, has both identified the sex of carers and related this to service provision.

Some of the first research which examined this

suggested that the home help services were provided more often when sons and husbands were the main carers for dependent people than when daughters and wives had taken on the responsibility (Hunt, 1970; Bristow, 1981; Charlesworth et al, 1983; Bebbington and Davies, 1983), regardless of the degree of dependency of the cared-for person. Wright, in her study of single (unmarried) carers also suggested that carer daughters were less likely to be provided with domiciliary help than carer sons (Wright, 1983).

By contrast, one study revealed that day-care facilities appeared to be more likely to be offered to female carers (other than spouses) than male carers (Charlesworth et al, 1983). In practice, however, this was temporary relief for daughters carrying a great burden caring for elderly parents as day care was provided to female carers at a much later stage in the onset of dependency than when men were main carers. Charlesworth et al conclude that:

> The allocation of service support reflects needs but is mediated by a set of expectations which assume that it is appropriate for women to undertake a heavier burden of care than might be expected of men. (p.33)

More recently Arber et al (1988) and Arber and Gilbert (1989) have demonstrated that it is not sex, per se, which influences service provision but rather, as indicated above, the inter-relationships between sex of the carer, sex of the cared-for person, household composition and size, the carer's relationship to the cared-for person, the carer's relationship to the labour market, and the substitutability of the service itself. Thus, for example, when the degree of the elderly person's disability was taken into account younger, lone, female carers, contrary to Wright's (1983) findings, received no less support than lone male carers. However *married* women carers under 65 received the lowest levels of domestic and personal health care support. What this analysis also showed, which previous researchers had not noticed, was the extent to which elderly couples ended up supporting one another.

Arber et al (1988) found that, controlling for disability, elderly men and women who lived alone were over five times more likely to receive a home help service than were elderly married couples, regardless of who was the carer.

In sum, this work suggests that, at least in regard to those who care for the elderly, service receipt does not discriminate against women, as such, but does discriminate against married women under the age of 65. Given this, it is not perhaps such a surprise to find that for families supporting a child with disabilities the supply of certain types of statutory support is at an even lower level than that provided for elderly people (Wilkin, 1979; Glendinning, 1985). Bristow (1981) has argued that parents caring for a disabled child are very unlikely to be receiving the home help service and much less likely than other carers to be visited by a district nurse, findings confirmed by the OPCS disability surveys. For example, less than one per cent of parents of disabled children in the survey had used the home help or laundry service in the 12 months prior to being interviewed (Meltzer, Smyth and Robus, 1989). Yet 7 per cent of parents of the most severely disabled children who identified a need for additional services felt that they needed a home help service, while 17 per cent thought that a laundry service was needed. The need for home help support was also closely related to the age of the child, parents of the youngest children being more likely to identify the need. Health visitors were more often involved in supporting parents but not at the levels one might have expected. Only two-thirds of children aged 0–4 years and under a third of those in the severest disability categories had seen a health visitor in the previous 12 months. The most severely disabled children were more likely than the rest to have been visited by a community nurse, but even here, the general level of provision was low (16 per cent of those in severity categories 9–10 and 5 per cent overall) compared with that to adults with disabilities (55 per cent of those in categories 9–10 and 16 per cent overall). Yet among parents of the most severely disabled children who were able to identify unmet needs the community nursing service was one of the most important.

Before moving on it is probably worth pointing out that, although there are strong indications that service provision is related to household composition and the sex of the main carer, we cannot be entirely sure that this reflects only service providers' priorities. Research on the carers of elderly, mentally infirm people (Levin et al, 1983) suggests that the beliefs and attitudes of carers may also play an important part both in the seeking of support and in acceptance of it when offered.

Arber et al (1988), similarly, point out that the carer and the cared-for person may influence what services are actually used:

> The provision of personal health and hygiene services is related to the assessment of need by health professionals, which take into account the characteristics of the carer and the relationship between the carer and the cared for, as well as the wishes of the principal carer and of the elderly person … .Thus, actual receipt is the result of the interrelationship of decisions made by providers, carers and the elderly person. We have no knowledge from the GHS of the carer's or the elderly person's preferred form of support. (pp.170-1)

In the first edition of the book it was pointed out that only research which addressed the needs of both carers and cared-for people and which examined the attitudes and policies of service providers would resolve this question. Progress in this direction has been made with research on non-elderly spouse carers (Parker, 1989) which illustrates the 'negotiation' that goes on between the carer and the cared-for person and how this influences attitudes towards service receipt. This study has also shown how younger female carers' needs cannot be met by conventional services; they feel that they need services not to replace their own usual domestic labour (i.e. home help, meals-on-wheels) but to replace their disabled or ill husband's usual domestic labour (e.g. house painting, garden maintenance). What both male and female carers needed, however, was a replacement for their *un*usual domestic labour (i.e. providing intensely personal, physical care for their partner).

Research on the attitudes and policies of service providers and how these tally with the views of carers about the services they receive is also now underway (Twigg, 1989c) and will enhance our understanding of the negotiations that go on between the two parties.

(11)

Short-stay residential care

Short-stay residential care, provided by hospitals, hostels and other residential establishments, is used to give short breaks to dependent people and their carers. Usually, such arrangements are relatively infrequent (once a year) allowing carers to go away on holiday; occasionally, they are part of a rotating or phased care scheme; very occasionally, they are available 'on demand' when carers can no longer continue unsupported.

The provision of short-term care for elderly people in local authority residential accommodation has grown substantially over the past fifteen years, although, until recently, little was known about the nature or impact of this increase or about 'how short-stay care fitted into the general pattern of care for the elderly' (Allen, 1983). As well as this increased use of short-stay care, there appear to have been changes in the reasons for which it is used. Relief of carers, whether on a once-a-year basis or as part of rotating or phased care, has become more explicitly important in local authority policy, and some authorities have reduced the number of beds they have available for holidays for elderly people themselves.

Unfortunately, it is not at all clear that this increased use of short-stay care benefits either the old people already in the homes used by short-stay clients or the short-stay clients themselves. In addition, while the 'main beneficiaries of short-stay residential care for the elderly [are] undoubtedly the carers of elderly people in the community' for many 'it was a poor substitute for permanent care' (Allen, 1983 p.173), or better domiciliary services. As Allen concludes, an offer of short-stay residential care was, in some cases, less appropriate than would have been 'some provision or increase of community care, long-stay care, psychiatric or geriatric assessment, long-term support for the carer, or the provision or increase of day care....' (p.184).

Indeed, the short-fall in provision of statutory services for those caring for elderly people might 'lead to more demand for both short-stay and long-stay residential care than would otherwise be necessary', (p.185).

While short-stay residential care for elderly people

provided some relief for carers, then, it was not necessarily the most appropriate or efficient way of giving support. Moreover, in some cases, especially with elderly people suffering from dementia or when care was phased or rotating, the elderly person might return home more confused or difficult to care for than before the care placement.

Short-term residential care for mentally-handicapped children and adults, as conventionally provided, does not appear to meet either parents' or children's needs (Oswin, 1981). The majority of parents, when asked if they would like to be provided with short-term care facilities, indicate that they would not (Baldwin, 1976, cited in Philp and Duckworth, 1982; Carey, 1982). However, at least some of this reluctance to consider short-term care may be due to lack of information about its nature and the difficulty parents sometimes encounter in making arrangements (Malin, 1982). The place where short-term care is provided also appears to influence parents' reactions; parents of mentally handicapped adults in one study were happier with provision at hostels or on ATC holidays than they were with provision in hospitals (City of Bradford MDC, SSD 1983). Less formal, more readily available provision in specialist units (eg. Honeylands) appears to be more acceptable to parents (Goddard and Rubissow, 1977).

Even though short-term care, in its usual form, may not meet informal carers' real needs for support, it does provide some respite. However, evidence suggests that access to short-term care is not necessarily determined by need. Among the elderly, for example, short-term care may be less likely to go to those whose families have taken on the responsibility of caring (Bergmann et al, 1978), or may be provided at a later stage in dependency (Charlesworth et al, 1983). Where children with disabilities are concerned, the provision of short-term care may be crisis-oriented rather than part of on-going support (Wilkin, 1979). As with domiciliary and day-care services, there is some evidence that the sex of the main informal carer may influence whether or not, and at what stage of dependency, short-term residential care is provided (Charlesworth et al, 1983).

Cash benefits and support

A third form of 'conventional' support for carers is money. However, only one state benefit exists specifically to support informal carers and compensate them for loss of employment: the Invalid Care Allowance (ICA). Until recently, the stringent criteria applied to receipt of the ICA, and the disenfranchisement of all married women carers from receipt, meant that it reached very few informal carers. The EOC estimated that in 1979 only 0.5 per cent of informal carers were receiving ICA (EOC, 1982). The numbers receiving this benefit now are around 100,000, a number that represents, perhaps, 10 per cent of those carers who might be entitled to ICA purely on the basis of the number of hours for which they care (although this proportion does include elderly carers who are *not* entitled to ICA). Obviously, benefits paid to dependent people, or intended for their use, may be available to those who care for them. As Baldwin et al (1983) pointed out, benefits such as the Mobility and Attendance Allowances, although not intended as income replacement for the parents of disabled children, are likely to be used as such. This is especially the case when parents are more restricted in their employment opportunities than parents of normal children.

As with ICA, there is little evidence about how other benefits received by, or on behalf of, dependent people might help informal carers. Indeed, there is little evidence about the relationship between money generally and the duration or quality of care. Some commentators have already pointed to the link between income and dependency in old age (see chapter 1); similar links undoubtedly exist between income and dependency in other age groups. Recent exploratory work on the financial circumstances of carers (Glendinning, 1988 and 1989) has started to illuminate some of these issues. This work demonstrates, in particular, the crucial importance of household size and composition in determining the living standards of both carer and cared-for person. Some carers who were not in paid work were financially dependent on the cared-for person and his or her income, including benefits. This is an area which remains to be explored on a larger scale.

The Effectiveness of Conventional Services

The main aims in policy terms of providing services to dependent people (and, by default, their carers), whether explicit or implicit, are: keeping them out of institutional care and hence saving money; ensuring a reasonable standard of care; and keeping recipients well and happy. To what extent are these goals presently met by conventional health and social services? As with other questions raised in this review, answers must be sought from a variety of sources.

For dependent people who live alone, the way in which the receipt of services keeps them out of residential care is direct and unequivocal. For those who live with others, the relationship between service provision and continued care in the community is mediated through their carer, usually by reducing stress and the physical burden of care. For example, the interviewers and psychiatrists involved in Levin's study of those caring for elderly, mentally-infirm people at home were in no doubt that domiciliary, day-care and relief-care services 'promoted the capacity of the supporters to continue to care' (Levin et al, 1983, p 236). Home help services, community nursing, day and relief care, and receipt of the attendance allowance all reduced measurable strain on carers over a 12-month period. Receipt of home help services, particularly, appeared to reduce the likelihood of the elderly person's entering permanent residential care.

Gilhooly's work, also with carers of elderly, mentally-infirm people, offers a different perspective on this relationship (Gilhooly, 1986). While receipt of the home help service and of community nursing appeared to improve carers' morale and/or mental health, it did not affect carers' *attitudes* towards residential care for the person they were supporting. While most valued the services they received, and many said that they could not have continued caring without them (this was especially the case with day care), they would still have preferred residential care for their elderly relative, if given free choice.

One suspects that the same might have been true of Nissel and Bonnerjea's respondents who had been offered phased or rotating short-term care for their elderly relatives. These particular dependants 'needed almost continuous care and attention' and phased care had apparently been 'used to keep the carer from giving up' (Nissel and Bonnerjea, 1982, p 25).

It appears then that, where support services are available to those caring for elderly people, especially those who are mentally infirm, they do prevent or delay admission to residential care. However, they seem to do this by preventing carers 'giving up' rather than by providing what carers actually want. We have no evidence that the quality of caring prolonged in this way is adequate, nor what the long-term effect on the carer may be. However, for the majority of informal carers the issue of effectiveness of service provision is a meaningless one because they receive little or no statutory support at all. Further, this work is based on small samples of people caring for particular types of dependent people.

Evaluation of the effectiveness of service provision to those caring for children or adults with disabilities cannot be based on the same criteria used to evaluate services to the elderly, i.e. the delay or avoidance of admission to residential care. Very few long-term residential care places are available for these groups and, in any case, only a very small minority of carers would ever wish their dependants to enter such care. Evaluation of those services which are provided (and as we have seen these are limited) should, therefore, concentrate more on the reduction of stress in informal carers and enhanced quality of care in the home. Little evidence along these lines is available to date.

New Developments in Community Care Services

Recognition of the growing number of people requiring care in the 'community', promptings from central government, provisions for joint financing of projects which help transfer people from hospital or institutional care to the community, have all led in the last few years to a proliferation of schemes which have as their aim the promotion of 'community care'. As might be expected, such schemes reflect, in their diversity, the wide range of interpretations of the concept of 'community care' noted in the Introduction. Inevitably, many of these schemes, for example those set up to help move people out of long term institutional care, do not concern us here. The following section concentrates only on initiatives intended to keep people out of hospitals or institutions and to maintain them in their own homes in the community. Only schemes which, by design or as a side effect, had an impact on carers, are considered.

It would be impractical to review individually all the projects and schemes developed over the past few years. Not all have been reported and details of individual schemes often owe more to local variation in needs and history than to any underlying rationale. In any case, others have already catalogued some of these developments (Fennel, 1982; DHSS/SWSDG, 1983; Ward, 1982; Thornton and Moore, 1980). Ideally the emphasis of this section would be on those projects and schemes which have been evaluated and, more particularly, those which have attempted to assess or measure impact on carers. Unfortunately, the absence of a rigorous evaluation element in many of these developments makes this impossible (Twigg, 1989b).

First, two major and some minor recent developments in service provision, which have as their aim the maintenance of 'community care', are examined.

'Community care' schemes

One of the difficulties with the provision of conventional services, as outlined earlier in this section, is organisational fragmentation. This makes it unlikely that any one professional can put together a 'package' of services which best meets the needs of dependent people and/or their carers. The Kent Community Care Project has attempted to solve this difficulty. The project, set up by Kent County Council social services department and monitored by the Personal Social Services Research Unit at the University of Kent, has provided a model of innovative community care which is being replicated in other parts of the country (Challis and Davies, 1980 and 1985; Davies and Challis, 1986; Chesterman et al, 1988).

Set in the context of a growing, and increasingly frail, elderly population in the seaside retirement towns of Kent, and a time of economic constraint on local authorities, the original project attempted:

> ... to mobilise, or indeed generate, extra help in the community to meet adequately the needs of some of the vulnerable elderly clients [of the social services department] requiring residential accommodation. (Challis and Davies, 1980)

This help generated from the community was to be used to fill gaps between the services already available to frail elderly people.

The main aim of the project was, thus, to maintain in the community elderly people who might otherwise have been obvious clients for residential care and, moreover, to do this at a cost lower than that of residential care.

The major methods adopted to help achieve this aim were individual case management by experienced local authority social workers, coupled with decentralised budget allocation (though not distribution). Social workers had complete responsibility 'for the co-ordination and development of care for the elderly people' (Challis and Davies, 1980). Control over the allocation of financial resources was crucial to success of the scheme, not only allowing use of existing services but also encouraging development of additional sources of help from the voluntary and informal sector.

> A contract would be negotiated with a member or members of the local community — or for that matter with an agency, profit making or otherwise — to provide certain services for a client at a given rate. These service providers or agents could then be paid directly for the tasks undertaken at the rate specified in the contract; payment being for the task and not an hourly rate. (Challis and Davies, 1980)

The social worker also ensured that other 'caring resources' were co-ordinated, the helpers filling in gaps between statutory provision.

The clients helped in the Kent scheme were, perhaps, atypical in that many of them had retired to the seaside town in which the project was based and had little or no family living near. Few had anyone who could be identified as a main carer. By contrast, a scheme established in Gateshead, on the same principles as the Kent scheme and evaluated by the same research team, aimed 'to complement help already available in the community and offer realistic and meaningful relief so as to consolidate informal care, rather than undermine it' (Challis et al, 1983). Gateshead is an area where elderly people are more likely to live near to, if not with, relatives. The social worker co-ordinates existing informal care and statutory services and fills gaps by recruiting 'care helpers'. The use of a decentralised budget has allowed aids not otherwise available to be bought and innovative day care, sometimes in the care helpers' own homes, to be provided (Challis et al, 1988).

Both schemes have kept frail, elderly people out of residential care and have improved their quality of life. Clients who might not have benefited from conventional services have been reached, and 'effective management of care resources' has been made possible. 'With devolved budgetary control, resources can be deployed more imaginatively, monitored more closely and interwoven flexibly with other forms of care both statutory and voluntary' (Challis et al, 1983). In addition, some of the burden of care previously carried by informal carers has been relieved.

The successful implementation of the Kent type of community care scheme in an area with a very different social composition is encouraging, suggesting that this type of scheme, carefully monitored and supervised, could be developed in other authorities.

Both schemes demonstrated some improvements in carers' well-being in the 'experimental' groups. In the Kent scheme there was a significant improvement in the carers' level of subjective burden (Challis and Davies, 1985) and in the Gateshead scheme in carers' 'lifestyle problems', 'mental health problems', 'level of strain' and 'expressed burden' (Challis et al, 1988). There are a number of points to be made here.

First, the apparently greater impact of the Gateshead scheme on carers may be due to the additional element of the 'care helpers', who were not present in the Kent scheme. These helpers seemed to perform a function much like that of care attendants (see below), who are known to meet carers' needs in some significant ways.

Secondly, in the Gateshead scheme comparisons were also made between those carers whose dependants had actually entered residential or hospital care and those who had not, regardless of whether they were in the 'experimental' group. In all aspects of carer outcomes, except 'mental health problems', the carers whose dependent person had gone into residential or hospital care appeared to have made *more* improvement. Thus, for example, the mean change in 'lifestyle problems' for the experimental group carers whose dependant had remained at home was –1.8 while for those whose dependant had entered care it was –3.4. In the control group the equivalent changes were –0.7 and –2.8. Not surprisingly, institutional care was less successful in reducing mental health problems relating to anxiety and guilt.

Thirdly, the Gateshead evaluation indicated that the 'experimental' intervention made no significant difference in the amount of care given and the Kent scheme showed no significant improvements in difficulties in carers' social lives, household routines, employment difficulties or financial difficulties.

Thus, while the experimental schemes undoubtedly benefited elderly people and kept them in the community for longer than would otherwise have been possible, it is not at all clear that any substantial benefit accrued to carers *despite* improvements in service inputs. Given the very high level of dependency of the elderly people involved, these findings are, perhaps, not so surprising. As the figures suggest, admission to residential care might well have been the only option which would have had any real impact on the carer. This, of course, echoes Levin et al's findings.

A number of issues about this intervention, *vis-a-vis* carers, thus remain. While there may be some relief to carers, it is also the case that some informal carers may become *more* involved, for longer periods, as a result of the scheme's intervention. Indeed, this is explicitly stated in an account of the Gateshead scheme (Challis et al, 1983). It is not evident, from available accounts of the schemes, that the full economic, social and psychological costs to informal carers involved in these schemes have been taken into account, particularly in relation to costs over time. It seems highly likely that carers who have their employment disrupted for, say, four years rather than one will incur greater costs over the long term (ie beyond the period of caring). Neither is it clear that informal carers' wishes and needs have been fully explored. For example, would informal carers involved in a community care scheme still prefer their dependent relative to enter residential care?

There also appears to be an underlying assumption in evaluation of the schemes that continuing care at home is necessarily preferable to residential care. While this *may* be so for most elderly people it is not clear that the issue of the appropriateness of continuing care in the community (Opit, 1977; DHSS, 1981; Nissel and Bonnerjea, 1982) has been adequately explored so far (see Finch 1984 and Dalley 1988 for critiques).

While 'Kent type' community care schemes do appear to offer a flexible and responsive approach to the needs of frail, elderly people, questions remain to be answered before they can be accepted as a panacea for the problems of caring for the growing elderly population.

One experimental question that remains is whether this model might benefit carers more if provided at a rather earlier stage in the cared-for person's dependency. Cost benefits to service providers would not be as likely in the short-term but very substantial effects, both to providers and to carers, might become evident over time.

The combination of individual case-management with decentralised budgeting may have applications for client groups other than the frail elderly. Less dependent elderly people, informal carers of disabled adults, families with disabled children, might all benefit from the close matching of needs and services made possible by this innovative approach.

Care attendant and intensive domiciliary care schemes

Schemes considered under this heading provide substitute or support care in the home of people with disabilities. They differ from more conventional domiciliary services, such as home help or district nursing, in that care can be provided at most hours of the day or night to suit the needs of the disabled person and his or her family.

Although the schemes work in much the same way, by providing help in the home of the dependent person with tasks not normally carried out by statutory helpers, their original aims differ considerably. 'Crossroads'-type care attendant schemes have been set up with the prime aim of relieving informal carers, while intensive domiciliary care schemes have more often been concerned with shortening hospital stays or keeping dependent people out of hospital or long-stay residential care altogether.

'Crossroads' care attendant schemes

The first 'Crossroads' care attendant scheme was established in Rugby in 1974:

> ...to provide care attendants to relieve the carers of severely physically disabled people. The care attendants, who are paid a standard wage, come at the time when the carers most need the relief, to act as a substitute for the carers to enable the carers to do whatever they need or want to do. Whilst in the home, the care attendant carries out whatever tasks would normally be done by the carer. (Bristow, 1981 p.7)

Thus, care attendants are not meant to replace, or make up for, more conventional, statutory, services but are intended solely to relieve informal carers.

The tasks undertaken by attendants include getting the disabled person up and dressed in the morning; helping them to bed at night; overnight stays to allow the main carer to sleep; regular visits during the day when the carer is out; specific 'daily living' tasks such as toileting, bathing, help with meals; providing a regular break to allow the main carer to go out; providing occasional holiday or weekend breaks; providing temporary or emergency help. Although all schemes have the same aim 'there is considerable diversity in the manner in which they are conceived, funded and organised' (Bristow, 1981, p.11), primarily because the initiative for starting a scheme may come from any of a number of sources, both voluntary and statutory.

Several Crossroads and Crossroads-like schemes have

been monitored and their impact on both carers and cared-for documented (Lovelock, 1981 a and b; Bristow, 1981; Bristow and Brenig-Jones, 1984; Cooper, 1986). However, although these accounts have included very detailed reports of what care attendants *did* for dependent people, the ways in which the impact of the schemes have been measured are general and often unsatisfactory. The schemes undoubtedly had beneficial outcomes for most dependent people, for example, allowing them to remain at home, increased companionship, reduced feelings of being a 'burden' to others, and so on. Similarly, most main carers in the studies reported the sense of relief the scheme had brought to them. Some had been able to remain at, or return to, work on a full-time basis; others were grateful for the periodic break from caring that the scheme afforded them. However, given the relatively low level of provision of conventional statutory services before the care attendant started to help the family, we do not know whether the benefits reported are specific to the particular scheme or whether any increase in service provision would have brought about similar benefits. A properly controlled experiment in service provision would need to be carried out to clarify this point.

Another important question about care attendant schemes, which is not answered by the published accounts, is whether statutory services are reduced or withdrawn when families have a care attendant. A few families in Bristow's study were interviewed soon after joining a scheme and again a year later. There was no evidence from this very small sample that use of the scheme had resulted in any reduction in statutory services. However, as provision of domiciliary services to disabled people who had informal carers was initially very low, this is perhaps not surprising. A more detailed examination of inter-relationships between the provision of conventional services and of care attendants is needed.

There have been recent moves to extend 'Crossroads' schemes to other groups, for example, to families caring for a person with mental handicaps (Bristow and Brenig-Jones, 1984). As Bristow (1981) has rightly pointed out, there is

> . . . no apparent reason why the expertise that the Crossroads organisation has developed should not be used to embrace other groups, since the philosophy of supporting the carer and maintaining people within the community is applicable to any group. (p.159-60)

However, she also points out that the needs of both carers and cared-for may differ from one dependency group to another and that 'pilot schemes helping one or more different client groups' should be developed 'using different organisational models, so that the advantages and disadvantages of different methods could be monitored and assessed' (p.160). Such pilot schemes should also be evaluated alongside *adequate* provision of statutory services.

Intensive domiciliary care

Intensive domiciliary care schemes, organised and run or funded by local authorities' social services departments or by health authorities, appear less likely to have the support of informal carers as their primary objective. The prevention or delay of admission to long-term residential or hospital care and the rehabilitation of patients discharged from hospital are cited more often in descriptions of such schemes (Schofield and Price, 1981a; Dexter, 1981; Crosby et al, 1982, 1983 and 1986), although relief of the burden of care may be an additional effect (Quelch, 1981). These schemes also tend to provide support on a short-term basis, aiming to bring recipients to a stage where they are sufficiently independent to cope with only standard statutory services.

Few of these schemes appear to have been rigorously evaluated, while one that did include an element of evaluation has not yet considered economic, social or psychological effects on informal carers (Crosby et al). The service studied did succeed in maintaining elderly mentally ill people who lived alone, or with elderly carers in the community, longer than similar elderly people who did not receive the service. It also appeared to reduce their use of day care and in-patient hospital care, home help services and meals-on-wheels. It is not entirely clear whether this reduced input of conventional services reflected a lower level of need in the intensive care group or the withdrawal of services *because* intensive domiciliary care was being provided. Intuitively, one would expect need to be reduced in the intensive care group, but the 'trade-off' between existing services and the new one were not explored sufficiently to confirm this.

Given what we already know about the importance to informal carers of time *away* from their elderly mentally infirm dependants, we must suspect that this reduction in the use of day care and in-hospital care facilities might increase social and psychological cost for carers.

Sitting services

Another development, which provides relief to carers by taking over caring tasks in the home, is that of sitting services. These services for elderly or other dependent people are, as their name suggests, a more developed form of 'baby-sitting'. They are usually, though not always, established by voluntary organisations and provide volunteers to sit in, freeing the carers of dependent people for a few hours (Mullender, 1983; see also entries in voluntary organisations section of Ferlie, 1982, and DHSS/SWSDG, 1983). Such services differ from care attendant schemes in that they are less likely to provide intensive care on such a regular basis. They are essentially a way of providing an occasional few hours of respite rather than a form of substitute care. Sitting-in can, of course, play an important part by filling gaps between other services and some schemes have led to the development of other services such as day centres (Robinson and Luszczak, 1986; Linge, 1986) or 'fostering' (Thornton, 1989).

A less usual form of sitting-in is provided by a jointly funded service in Rochdale. This combines night nursing (provided by the health authority) and night sitting (arranged by the social services department). Sitters who are not qualified nurses provide a through the night presence, supervised by visits during the night from the nursing service. The service aims to provide carers with an undisturbed night's sleep or, in some cases, to support frail, elderly or handicapped people who live alone (Schofield and Price, 1981b).

Although reports of both day and night sitting services always mention the relief that informal carers experience when they start using a sitting service there appears to have been no careful assessment of this effect and no comparison with alternative forms of service. Neither is there any indication that a sitting service is what best meets carers' needs.

For example, Green (1986) points to some of the difficulties of sitting schemes including the difficulties of identifying clients, professionals' suspicion of them, and the generally inflexible nature of their organisation. May et al (1986), in their assessment of a sitting scheme which failed, describe how carers tended to see the presence of the volunteer sitters as an implicit criticism of their (the carers') own commitment. Few of the volunteers were prepared for the problems they would encounter with demented elderly people and had difficulty communicating with them. (See Thornton, 1989 and Twigg 1989b for a more detailed account of sitting services.)

New forms of respite care

The provision of residential respite care has developed in two quite distinct ways in recent years. First, there has been the development of specialist services and units. Secondly, relatively informal 'fostering' schemes have been developed using ordinary families and homes to provide care for dependent children or adults on a short-term basis.

Schemes in the first category, although all providing 'respite care', vary widely in details of their organisation as the literature indicates (Goddard and Rubissons, 1977; Cunliffe, 1981; Tidball, 1981; Liddiard, 1981; Drummond, 1982; Farnes, 1985; Brook and Jestice, 1986; Francis, 1986). Funding, organisation, the extent of informal carers' involvement, aims and intentions, all differ between schemes.

It is not evident that many of these projects have included an evaluative element which attempted to gauge effects on carers. However, as some of the schemes have been set up *by* carers or in response to their promptings it must be assumed that they meet some of their needs. Even so, such developments are not without their critics, especially when care is provided in 'units' which combine short-term and long-term residential care with other functions such as training (Gathercole 1979, cited in Ward 1982). Reports of schemes which *have* been evaluated suggest that carers appreciate the break from caring that these more specialised schemes offer, especially when respite care can be provided more or less 'on demand' (Green and Evans 1982).

Fostering and family placements for both adults and children with special needs are relatively new developments. Schemes specifically for elderly people have been reviewed by Thornton and Moore (1980), who identified 23 schemes, most of which included both long-term and short-term components. Almost all the schemes were run by social services departments although some were jointly financed with health authorities.

Although half of the schemes identified had relief of carers as their main aim, the study did not directly address the issue of impact on informal carers. A small number of carers were approached by the authors and all 'appeared to have confidence both in the efficiency of the scheme and the capabilities of the [substitute] carers...' (p.96). However, there was some evidence that relationships between the informal carers and those they cared for deteriorated when the client returned home. Some elderly people made unfavourable comparisons between the care and attention they normally received and that received during their placement away from home.

This finding raises similar questions about this form of respite care as were raised about traditional respite care in Allen's (1983) study of local authority provision. Both types are intended to relieve carers, and may be successful in doing so in the short term. However, there is a danger that, in the long run, the quality of carers' lives may be impaired or the duration of caring reduced.

As with other developments reviewed here, we do not know whether adequate domiciliary and day-care services would reduce much of the need for fostering services, whether fostering is most useful as an adjunct to services already available, or whether fostering reduces the need for more conventional provision.

Family placement and fostering for children with disabilities and adults with mental handicaps has also been developing over the past few years. This appears to be an increasingly popular service, especially among the parents of mentally handicapped children who welcome the more informal provision of respite care (Oswin 1981, Newcastle City Council, 1986).

Although the impetus for this type of provision came originally from voluntary organisations, many local authority social services departments have now established similar schemes. Such evidence as is available about parents' use of fostering schemes for children with disabilities indicates that the service is useful, fills a need and is preferred to more conventional respite care (Ward 1982).

Support Groups

All the provisions considered so far have been oriented towards relieving the physical burdens and constraints of caring for a dependent person. However, another recent development, support groups for people who are carers, has shown that the moral and emotional support generated by sharing feelings and experiences with others in the same position can also be valuable. Many of these groups have been established by carers themselves and by voluntary organisations but, again, local authority social services departments are beginning to be involved.

Some groups have been established for carers of one particular dependency group, for example, stroke patients (Herbert 1983, Wilkinson and Zaborski 1983) or dementia patients (Church and Linge 1982, Linge 1986). Others have encompassed a wide range of disabilities (Smith 1983).

Support groups vary considerably in their organisation; some are relatively formal and include an invited speaker at each meeting followed by discussion; some are wholly organised and run by parents; some have trained facilitators to help guide the group to explore sensitive issues. Most, however, appear to combine advice and information exchange with more experiential work. Some also provide practical support and relief, usually on a mutual basis, e.g. baby-sitting circles, weekend and holiday clubs.

Evaluation of such loosely constructed initiatives is notoriously difficult. Those groups which have attempted some evaluation report considerable satisfaction among members both with the provision of concrete advice and with the opportunity to share feelings which had previously been suppressed (Smith 1983, Church and Linge 1982, Pugh et al 1981, Holland and Hattersley 1980). However, such groups are not without their problems and may, in some circumstances, benefit service providers rather more than they benefit carers (Smith and Cantley, 1983a). Again, Twigg (1989b) provides a detailed account of initiatives of this sort.

Information

Surveys of carers have shown time and again that one of their prime needs is for information: about the cared-for person's diagnosis and prognosis; about services, aids and adaptations; about finances and benefits; and so on. Even small amounts of information can make a substantial difference to carers' lives and relationships with service providers (Parker, 1989) and there has been a flurry of initiatives in this area in recent years. Some carers' groups are established with the primary aim of providing information. In other settings, information giving or 'training' for carers may come about directly as a separate initiative from service providers (Saddington, 1984, Garland, 1985). More generally, information may be made available by voluntary organisations for members (e.g. Multiple Sclerosis Society, Parkinson's Disease Society) or by local authorities. Finally, the King's Fund Informal Caring Support Unit and the Health Education Authority have been instrumental in producing and promoting a number of publications specifically aimed at carers.

While all these sources of information undoubtedly represent an improvement on the past, there are two caveats to be made. First, the *timing* of information-giving is crucial to carers; finding out about attendance allowance and invalid care allowance years after becoming entitled is not an uncommon experience for carers. Secondly, unless information about services is backed up by their availability, carers can be deeply disappointed. As Twigg (1989b) has said:

> Although the provision of information is generally recognised as important in the support of carers, criticism has been levelled at some of the local initiatives which have been interpreted, in the absence of service development, as low-cost, tokenist responses to the problem. Some carers have complained that lists of services or voluntary sector 'phone numbers are of little use if the facilities are over-subscribed and support effectively unavailable. (p.28)

Summary and Conclusions

It is difficult to judge the impact of conventional health and welfare services on informal carers when such assessment has rarely been attempted by researchers or by those who provide the services. The evidence we are able to glean from various sources suggests that available services are likely to have little overall effect for informal carers. First, few dependent people who have informal carers appear to receive services and, when they do, such services are usually crisis-oriented rather than a part of long-term support. Secondly, the criteria by which services are allocated are often irrational (not allocated in relation to need) and discriminatory (not provided where female carers, particularly married women, are available).

Part of the reason for this ineffective provision must, of course, be financial. Given finite resources, service providers have chosen to support those people who have no one else to help them. It has been suggested that this is not, in fact, the most sensible use of services with some groups of dependent people (Opit 1977) and that resources might better be directed towards supporting informal carers.

Another part of the reason for the failure to help carers is the fragmented organisation of health and welfare services which makes it difficult for 'packages' of services to be put together to meet the needs of both dependent people and their carers.

It is difficult, then, to say what might be the most effective, and cost-effective, forms of support to carers and cared-for within services as they are organised at present. While there is some indication that the most welcome forms of support are those which release carers completely from the burden of care for a short time (e.g. day care, night sitting), much still remains to be discovered about the form of relief services which would best meet their needs. Moreover, research has told us little as yet about how cash benefits might function as part of a supporting package for carers.

Both growing concern about the number of elderly, particularly frail elderly, people to be cared for and an increasing awareness of the burden carried by informal carers have stimulated the development of new approaches to service provision and, indeed, of new services. Yet it appears, with one notable exception, that rigorous evaluation of these initiatives has not played a prominent part in their development. This lacuna leaves several important questions unanswered and seriously compromises claims made for these innovations concerning their effectiveness. Until innovative services are directly compared against *adequate* provision of existing services, and a full account of the costs and benefits to informal carers included in this comparison, these questions will remain unanswered.

Finally, we still do not know enough about the respective needs of carers and cared-for people and how these might sensibly be balanced.

References

ALLEN, Isobel C. (1983), *Short-stay residential care for the elderly*, Policy Studies Institute, London.

ARBER, S. and GILBERT, N. (1989), **Men: the forgotten carers**, *Sociology*, 23, 1: 111-118.

ARBER, S.; GILBERT, N. and EVANDROU, M. (1988), **Gender, household composition and receipt of domiciliary services by the elderly disabled**, *Journal of Social Policy*, 17, 2: 153-175.

ATKIN, K.; TWIGG, J.; and PERRING, C. (1989), **Evaluating services in support of informal carers**, in *SPRU and Informal Care*, University of York, Social Policy Research Unit.

AUDIT COMMISSION (1986), *Making a reality of community care*, HMSO, London.

AYER, S. and ALASZEWSKI, A. (1984), *Community care and the mentally handicapped: services for mothers and their mentally handicapped children*, Croom Helm, London.

BALDWIN, S.M. (1977), **Disabled children — counting the costs**, Disability Alliance, Pamphlet no.8, London.

BALDWIN, S.M. (1981), **The financial consequences of disablement in children: final report**, University of York, Social Policy Research Unit, Working Paper DHSS76.

BALDWIN, S.M. (1985), *The costs of caring*, Routledge & Kegan Paul, London.

BALDWIN, S.M. and GLENDINNING, C. (1983), **Employment, women and their disabled children** in Groves, D. and Finch, J. (eds) *A Labour of Love: Women, Work and Caring*, Routledge & Kegan Paul, London.

BALDWIN, S.M., GODFREY, C. and STADEN, F. (1983), **Childhood Disablement and Family Incomes**, *Epidemiology and Community Health*, 37: 187-195.

BALDWIN, S. and PARKER, G. (1989), **The Griffiths report on community care**, in Brenton, M. and Ungerson, C., (eds), *Social Policy Review*, 1988-9, Longman, Harlow.

BAYLEY, M. (1973), *Mental Handicap and Community Care*, Routledge and Kegan Paul, London.

BEBBINGTON, A.C. and DAVIES, B. (1983), **Equity and efficiency in the allocation of personal social services**, *Journal of Social Policy*, 12, 3: 309-30.

BERGMANN, K., FOSTER, E.M., JUSTICE, A.W. and MATTHEWS, V. (1978), **Management of the demented elderly patient in the community**, *British Journal of Psychiatry*, 132: 441-449.

BLAXTER, M. (1976), *The Meaning of Disability*, Heinemann, London.

BODKIN, C.M., PIGOTT, T.J. and MANN, J.R. (1982), **Financial burdens of childhood cancer**, *British Medical Journal, 284*: 1542-4.

BONE, M. and MELTZER, H. (1989), *The Prevalence of Disability Among Children*, HMSO, London.

BONNY, S. (1984), *Who Cares in Southwark?* Association of Carers.

BOWLING, A. (1984), **Caring for the elderly widowed: the burden on their supporters**, *British Journal of Social Work*, 14, 5: 435-55.

BRADSHAW, J. (1980), *The Family Fund: An Initiative in Social Policy*, Routledge & Kegan Paul, London.

BRADSHAW, J. and LAWTON, D. (1976), **Tracing the Causes of Stress in Families with Handicapped Children**, *British Journal of Social Work*, 8, 2: 181-192.

BRISTOW, A.K., (1981), *Crossroads Care Attendant Schemes: A Study of their Organisation and Working Practice and of the Families whom they Support*, Association of Crossroads Care Attendants Schemes, Rugby.

BRISTOW, A.K. and BRENIG-JONES, J. (n.d.), *An Appraisal of the Wirral Crossroads Care Attendant Scheme*, Association of Crossroads Care Attendant Schemes Ltd, Rugby.

BRODY, Elaine M. (1981), **'Women in the Middle' and Family Help to Older People**, *The Gerontologist,* 21, 5: 471-480.

BROOK, P and JESTICE, S. (1986), **Relief for the Demented and their Relatives**, *Geriatric Medicine*, June, pp 31-36.

BROWN, J. (1980), **The Normansfield Inquiry** in Brown, M. and Baldwin, S., (eds), *The Yearbook of Social Policy 1978*, Routledge and Kegan Paul, London.

BURTON, L. (1975), *The Family Life of Sick Children*, Routledge & Kegan Paul, London.

BYRNE, E.A. and CUNNINGHAM, C.C. (1985), **The Effects of Mentally Handicapped Children on Families**, *Journal of Child Psychology & Psychiatry*, 26, 6: 847- 864.

CAREY, Gwyneth E. (1982), **Community Care — Care by Whom? Mentally Handicapped Children Living at Home**, *Public Health*, 96: 269-278.

CARR, J. (1976), **Effect on the Family of a Child with Downs' Syndrome**, *Physiotherapy*, 62, 1: 20-23.

CARR, J., PEARSON, A. and HALLIWELL, M. (1983), *The GLC Spina Bifida Survey: Follow Up at 11 and 12 years*, St George's Hospital Medical School, University of London.

CARTWRIGHT, A., HOCKEY, L. and ANDERSON, J.L. (1973), *Life Before Death*, Routledge & Kegan Paul, London.

CENTRAL STATISTICAL OFFICE (1989), *Social Trends 19*, HMSO, London.

CHALLIS, D., CHESSUM, R., CHESTERMAN, J., LUCKETT, R. and WOODS, B. (1988), **Community Care for the Frail Elderly: an Urban Experiment**, *British Journal of Social Work*, 18, supplement: 13-42.

CHALLIS, D. and DAVIES, B. (1980), **A New Approach to Community Care for the Elderly**, *British Journal of Social Work*, 10: 1-18.

CHALLIS, D. and DAVIES, B. (1985), **Long Term Care for the Elderly: the Community Care Scheme**, *British Journal of Social Work*, 15: 563-579.

CHARLESWORTH, A, WILKIN, D. and DURIE, A. (1983), *Carers and Services: a Comparison of Men and Women Caring for Dependent Elderly People*, University of Manchester, Departments of Psychiatry and Community Medicine.

CHALLIS, D., LUCKETT, R. and CHESSUM, R. (1983), **A New Life at Home**, *Community Care*, no. 455, 24/3/83.

CHESTERMAN, J., CHALLIS, D. and DAVIES, B. (1988), **Long-term Care at Home for the Elderly: a Four Year Follow Up**, *British Journal of Social Work*, 18, supplement: 43-54.

CHETWYND, J.S. (1983), **Costing the Role of the Principal Care-giver in the Domiciliary Care of the Elderly**, *Community Health Studies*, 7, 2: 146-8.

CHETWYND, J. (1985), **Factors Contributing to Stress on Mothers Caring for an Intellectually Handicapped Child**, *British Journal of Social Work*, 15: 295-304.

CHURCH, M. and LINGE, K.M. (1982), **Dealing with Dementia in the Community**, *Community Care*, no. 439, 25/11/82: 20-21.

CITY OF BRADFORD METROPOLITAN DISTRICT COUNCIL SOCIAL SERVICES DEPARTMENT (1983), *The Future Accommodation Needs of Mentally Handicapped People Presently Living in the Community*, Clearing House for Social Services Research, University of Birmingham, no. 2.

CLARKSON, S.E., CLARKSON, J.E., DITTMER, I.E., FLETT, R., LINSELL, C., MULLEN, P. and MULLIN, B. (1986), **Impact of a Handicapped Child on Mental Health of Parents**, *British Medical Journal*, 293: 1395-1397.

COOKE, K. (1982), **1970 Birth Cohort — 10 Year Follow-up Study: Interim Report**, University of York, Dept. of Social Policy and Social Work. Social Policy Research Unit Working Paper DHSS 108.

COOPER, M., (1986), **On the Right Road**, *Community Care*, 14/8/86: 24-25.

CRAIG, John (1983), **The Growth of the Elderly Population**, *Population Trends*, no. 32, OPCS, London.

CREEK, G., MOORE, M., OLIVER, M., SALISBURY, V., SILVER, V. and ZARB, G. (n.d.), *Personal and Social Implications of Spinal Cord Injury: a Retrospective Study*, Thames Polytechnic.

CROSBY, C., COPELAND, J.R.M., EL ASSRA, A. and STEVENSON, R.C. (1982), *The Age Concern Liverpool Intensive Domiciliary Care Scheme for Elderly Mentally Ill People*, University of Liverpool, Institute of Human Ageing.

CROSBY, C., COPELAND, J.R.M., EL ASSRA, A., STEVENSON, R.C. and BLAKE, A. (1983), *The Intensive Domiciliary Care Scheme for Elderly Mental Ill People: a Second Report*, University of Liverpool, Institute of Human Ageing.

CROSBY, C., COPELAND, J.R.M., EL ASSRA, A. and STEVENSON, R.C. (1986), *The Liverpool Intensive Domiciliary Care Scheme for Elderly Mental Ill People, 1981-1986*, University of Liverpool, Institute of Human Ageing.

CUNLIFFE, A. (1981), **Joint Action**, *Health and Social Services Journal*, 28/8/81: 1044-1046.

DALLEY, G. (1988), *Ideologies of Caring: Rethinking Community and Collectivism*, Macmillan Education, London.

DAVIES, B. and CHALLIS, D. (1986), *Matching Resources to Needs in Community Care*, Gower, Aldershot.

DAVIS, Linda, J. (1981), **Service Provision and the Elderly: Attitudes of Three Generations of Urban Women**, *The Occupational Therapy Journal of Research*, 1, 1: 32-52.

DEXTER, M. (1981), **Intensive Care at Home**, *Health and Social Services Journal*, 13/2/81: 170.

DHSS SOCIAL WORK SERVICE DEVELOPMENT GROUP (1983), *Supporting the Informal Carers: Information (initiatives, literature and contacts)*, DHSS, London.

DRUMMOND, P. (1982), **At Home on the Harrow Road**, *Health and Social Services Journal*, 17/8/82: 976.

EQUAL OPPORTUNITIES COMMISSION (1980), *The Experience of Caring for Elderly and Handicapped Dependants; Survey Report,* EOC, Manchester.

EQUAL OPPORTUNITIES COMMISSION (1981), *Behind Closed Doors*, Equal Opportunities Commission, Manchester.

EQUAL OPPORTUNITIES COMMISSION (1982), *Caring for the Elderly and Handicapped: Community Care Policies and Women's Lives*, EOC, Manchester.

EVANDROU, M., ARBER, S., DALE, A. and GILBERT, G.N. (1986), **Who Cares for the Elderly? Family Care Provision and Receipt of Statutory Service** in Phillipson, C., Bernard, M. and Strang, P., (eds), *Dependency and Interdependency in Old Age*, Croom Helm, London.

FARRIES, J. (1985), **Giving the Carers a Much Needed Break**, *Health Service Journal*, 8/8/85: 986-987.

FENGLER, A. P. and GOODRICH, N. (1979), **Wives of Elderly Disabled Men: the Hidden Patients**, *The Gerontologist*, 19, 2: 175-183.

FENNELL, G. (ed) (1982), *DHSS Seminar — Support for Elderly People Living in the Community. Synopsis of Research Funded by DHSS, DoE and Other Agencies*, School of Economic and Social Studies, UEA, Norwich.

FERLIE, E. (1982), *Sourcebook of Innovations in the Community Care of the Elderly*, Personal Social Services Research Unit, University of Kent at Canterbury.

FINCH, J. (1984), **Community Care: Developing Non-sexist Alternatives**, *Critical Social Policy*, 3, 3: 6-18.

FINCH, J. (1987), **Family Obligations and the Life Course**, in Bryman, B., Bytheway, B., Allatt, P. and Keil, T., (eds), *Rethinking the Life Cycle,* Macmillan, London.

FINCH, J. and GROVES, D. (1980), **Community Care and the Family: a Case for Equal Opportunities**, *Journal of Social Policy*, 9, 4: 487-511.

FINCH, J. and GROVES, D., (eds) (1983), *A Labour of Love: Women, Work and Caring*, Routledge & Kegan Paul, London.

FRANCIS, W. (1986), **Time to Draw Breath**, *Community Care Supplement*, 30/10/86: vii-viii.

GARLAND, J. (1985), **Adaptation Skills in the Elderly, Their Supporters and Carers**, *British Journal of Medical Psychology*, 58: 267-274.

GILHOOLY M. (1982), **Social Aspects of Senile Dementia**, in Taylor, R and Gilmore, A (eds), *Current Trends in Gerontology: Proceedings of the 1980 Conference of the British Society of Gerontology*, Gower, Aldershot.

GILHOOLY, M. (1984), **The Impact of Caregiving on Caregivers: Factors Associated with the Psychological Well-being of People Supporting a Dementing Relative in the Community**, *British Journal of Medical Psychology*, 57: 35-44.

GILHOOLY, M. (1986), **Senile Dementia: Factors Associated with Caregivers' Preference for Institutional Care**, *British Journal of Medical Psychology*, 59: 165-171.

GILLEARD, C.J., WATT, G. and BOYD, W.D. (1981), **Problems of Caring for the Elderly Mentally Infirm at Home**. Paper presented at the Twelfth International Congress of Gerontology, July 12th-17th, Hamburg, W. Germany.

GILLEARD, C.J., GILLEARD, E., GLEDHILL, K. and WHITTICK, J. (1984), **Caring for the Elderly Mentally Infirm at Home: A Survey of the Supporters**, *Journal of Epidemiology and Community Health*, 38: 319-325.

GLEDHILL, K.J., MACKIE, J.E. and GILLEARD, C.J. (1982), **A Comparison of Problems and Coping Reported by Supporters of Elderly Day Hospital Patients with Similar Ratings Provided by Nurses**. Paper presented to the British Psychological Society Annual Conference, April 1982.

GLENDINNING, C. (1983), *Unshared Care*, Routledge and Kegan Paul, London.

GLENDINNING, C. (1985), *A Single Door*, George Allen & Unwin, London.

GLENDINNING, C. (1988), **Dependency and Interdependency: the Incomes of Informal Carers and the Impact of Social Security**, in Baldwin, S., Parker, G. and Walker, R., (eds), *Social Security and Community Care*, Avebury, Aldershot.

GLENDINNING, C. (1989), **The Financial Needs and Circumstances of Informal Carers: Final Report,** University of York, Social Policy Research Unit Working Paper DHSS 529.

GODDARD, J. and RUBISSOW, J. (1977), **Meeting the Needs of Handicapped Children and their Families. The Evolution of Honeylands: a Family Support Unit, Exeter**, *Child: Care, Health & Development*, 3: 261-273.

GOFFMAN, E. (1968), *Asylums*, Doubleday and Co. New York.

GOLDBERG, D.P. (1972), *The Detection of Psychiatric Illness by Questionnaire*, Oxford University Press, London.

GREEN, H. (1988), *General Household Survey 1985: Informal Carers*, HMSO, London.

GREEN, J. (1986), **A Break or a Breakdown?**, *Community Care*, 15/5/85: 22- 24.

GREEN, J.M. and EVANS, R.C. (1982), **Honeylands' Role in the Pre-school Years I. Developing a Relationship**, *Child: Care, Health and Development*, 8: 21- 78.

GREENGROSS, Sally (1982), **Caring for the Carers,** in Glendenning, F., (ed.), *Care in the Community: Recent Research and Current Projects*, Beth Johnson Foundation, Stoke.

GRIFFITHS, R. (1988), *Community Care: an Agenda for Action*, HMSO, London.

HALSEY, A.H., (ed.) (1972), *Trends in British Society since 1900*, Macmillan, London.

HARRIS, A. (1971), *Handicapped and Impaired in Great Britain*, HMSO, London.

HASKEY, J. (1987), **Trends in Marriage and Divorce in England and Wales 1837- 1987**, *Population Trends*, no 48, OPCS, London.

HERBERT, Y., WILLISON, J. and ZABORSKI, A. (1983), **Strength in Sadness**, *Social Work Today*, 15, 7: 14-15.

HIRST, M. (1982), **Young Adults with Disabilities and their Families,** University of York, Social Policy Research Unit, Working Paper DHSS 112.

HIRST, M.A. (1983), **Evaluating the Malaise Inventory: An Item Analysis**, *Social Psychiatry*, 18: 181-184.

HIRST, M. (1984), **Moving On: Transfer from Child to Adult services for Young People with Disabilities,** University of York, Social Policy Research Unit, Working Paper DHSS 190.

HIRST, M.A. and BRADSHAW, J.R. (1983), **Evaluating the Malaise Inventory: A Comparison of Measures of Stress**, *Journal of Psychosomatic Research*, 27: 193-199.

HOLLAND, J.M. and HATTERSLEY, J. (1980), **Parent Support Groups for the Families of Mentally Handicapped Children**, *Child: Care, Health and Development*, 6: 165-73.

HUNT, A. (1968), *A Survey of Women's Employment*, HMSO, London.

HUNT, A. (1978), *The Elderly at Home*, OPCS Social Survey Division, HMSO, London.

HYMAN, M. (1977), *The Extra Costs of Disabled Living*, DIG/ ARC, London.

ISAACS, B., LIVINGSTON, M. and NEVILLE, Y. (1972), *Survival of the Unfittest: A Study of Geriatric Patients in Glasgow*, Routledge & Kegan Paul, London.

JAEHNIG, W. (1979), *A Family Service for the Mentally Handicapped*, Fabian Society Tract, no. 460, Fabian Society, London.

JOHNSON, M. (1983), **Independence and Old Age: The Contribution of the Voluntary Sector**, *Research, Policy and Planning*, 1, 1: 12-15.

JONES, D.A. and VETTER, N.J. (1984), **A Survey of Those Who Care for the Elderly at Home: Their Problems and Their Needs**, *Social Science and Medicine*, 19, 5: 511-514.

JONES, K. (1960), *Mental Health and Social Policy, 1845-1959*, Routledge and Kegan Paul, London.

JONES, K., BROWN, J. and BRADSHAW, J. (1978), *Issues in Social Policy*, (1st edn), Routledge and Kegan Paul, London.

JOSHI, H. (1987), **The Cost of Caring**, in Glendinning, C. and Millar, J., (eds), *Women and Poverty*, Wheatsheaf Books, Brighton.

JOWELL, T. and PRIOR, D. (1989), **Caring for the Carers**, *Insight*, 2/5/89: 16-18.

KAY, D.W.K., BERGMANN, K., FOSTER, E.M., McKECHNIC, A and ROTH, M. (1970), **Mental Illness and Hospital Usage in the Elderly: A Random Sample Followed Up,** *Comparative Psychiatry*, 2: 26-35.

KING'S FUND INFORMAL CARING PROGRAMME (1988), *Action for Carers: A Guide to Multi-Disciplinary Support at Local Level.*

KINSELLA, G.J. and DUFFY, F.D. (1979), **Psychosocial Readjustment in the Spouses of Aphasic Patients**, *Scandinavian Journal of Rehabilitation Medicine*, 11: 129-32.

LAND, H. (1978), **Who Cares for the Family**, *Journal of Social Policy*, 7, 3: 257-284.

LAWTON, D. and PARKER, G. (forthcoming), **A Typology of Caring: Secondary Analysis of the 1985 General Household Survey,** University of York, Social Policy Research Unit.

LEAT, Diana (1983), *Getting to Know the Neighbours: A Pilot Study of the Elderly and Neighbourly Helping*, PSI, London.

LEVIN, E., SINCLAIR, I. and GORBACH, P. (1983), **The Supporters of Confused Elderly People at Home: Extract from the Main Report,** National Institute for Social Work Research Unit, London.

LEWIS, J. and MEREDITH, B. (1988), *Daughters Who Care: Daughters Caring for Mothers at Home*, Routledge, London.

LIDDIARD, R. (1981), **Preserving Their Lifestyle**, *Health and Social Services Journal*, 25/9/81: 1181.

LINGE, K. (1986), **Setting Up a Relative Support Group**, *Community Care Supplement*, 30/10/86: v-vii.

LIVINGSTON, M.G., BROOKS, D.N. and BOND, M.R. (1985), **Three Months After Severe Head Injury: Psychiatric and Social Impact on Relatives**, *Journal of Neurology Neurosurgery & Psychiatry*, 48: 870-875.

LOVELOCK, R. (1981a), **... Friends in Deed: Three Care Attendant Schemes for the Younger Physically Disabled in Hampshire**, Social Services Research & Intelligence Unit, Dept. of Social Studies, Portsmouth Polytechnic.

LOVELOCK, R. (1981b), **Caring at Home**, *Health & Social Services Journal*, 31/7/81: 925-7.

McKAY, B., NORTH, N. and MURRAY-SYKES, K. (1983), **The Effects on Carers of Hospital Admission of the Elderly**, *Nursing Times*, 30/11/83: 42-43.

MACLEAN, M. and EEKELAAR, J. (1983), *The Financial Consequences of Divorce*, Centre for Socio-legal studies, Wolfson College, Oxford.

MALIN, N.A. (1982), **Short Term Care for Mentally Handicapped People**, Mental Handicap, 10, 3, 77, 78, 93.

MARTIN, J., MELTZER, H. and ELLIOT, D. (1988), *The Prevalence of Disability Among Adults*, HMSO, London.

MARTIN, J. and ROBERTS, C. (1984), *Women and Employment*, HMSO, London.

MARTIN, J. and WHITE A. (1988), *The Financial Circumstances of Disabled Adults Living in Private Households*, HMSO, London.

MARTIN, J., WHITE, A. and MELTZER, H. (1989), *Disabled Adults: Services, Transport and Employment*, HMSO, London.

MAY, D., McKEGANEY, N. and FLOOD, M. (1986), **Extra Hands or Extra Problems?**, *Nursing Times*, 8/9/86: 35-38.

MAYNARD, A. and SMITH, J.C.C. (1983), *The Elderly: Who Cares? Who Pays?*, Nuffield/York Portfolios: No.1, Nuffield Provincial Hospitals Trust.

MELTZER, H., SMYTH, M. and ROBUS, N. (1989), *Disabled Children: Services, Transport and Education*, HMSO, London.

MORONEY, R.M. (1976), *The Family and the State: Considerations for Social Policy*, Longman, London.

MORRIS, P. (1969) *Put Away*, Routledge & Kegan Paul, London.

MULLENDER, A. (1983), **Someone to Look after Grandma**, *Community Care*, 15/9/83.

NATIONAL AUDIT OFFICE (1987), *Community Care Developments*, HMSO, London.

NEWCASTLE CITY COUNCIL (1986), *Respite Care and Mental Handicap in Newcastle: An Evaluation of the FACE and STOP Schemes*, City of Newcastle Policy Services and Social Services Department.

NISSEL, M. (1984), **The Family Costs of Looking After Handicapped Elderly Relatives**, *Ageing and Society*, 4, 2: 185-204.

NISSEL, M. and BONNERJEA, L. (1982), *Family Care of the Handicapped Elderly: Who Pays?*, Policy Studies Institute, London.

NISW (National Institute for Social Work)/WAGNER, G. (Chair) (1988), *Residential Care: A Positive Choice*, HMSO, London.

ODDY, M., HUMPHREY, M. and UTTLEY, D. (1978), **Stresses Upon the Relatives of Head Injured Patients**, *British Journal of Psychiatry*, 133: 507-13.

OLIVER, J. (1983), **The Caring Wife** in Finch, J. and Groves, D., *A Labour of Love: Women, Work and Caring*, Routledge and Kegan Paul, London.

OPCS (1989), *General Household Survey 1986*, HMSO, London.

OPIT, L.J. (1977), **Domiciliary Care for the Elderly Sick — Economy or Neglect?**, *British Medical Journal*, 1: 30-33.

OSWIN, M. (1981), *Issues and Principles in the Development of Short-term Residential Care for Mentally Handicapped Children*, Kings Fund Centre, London.

PARKER, G. (1985), *With Due Care and Attention: A Review of Research on Informal Care*, (1st edition) Family Policy Studies Centre Occasional Paper No.2, London.

PARKER, G. (forthcoming), **They're got their own lives to lead: carers and dependent people talking about family and neighbourhood help**, in Hutton, J., Hutton, S., Pinch, T., and Shiell, A (eds), *Dependency to Enterprise*, Routledge, London

PARKER, G. (1989a), **A study of non-elderly spouse carers: final report,** University of York, Social Policy Research Unit Working Paper, DHSS 501.

PARKER, G. (1989b) **The same difference? The experiences of men and women caring for a spouse with a disability or chronic illness**, paper given at Social Policy Association Conference, University of Bath, July 1989.

PENTOL, A. (1983), **Cost Bearing Burdens**, *Health and Social Service Journal*, 8/9/83.

PERRING, C. (1989) **Families caring for those diagnosed as mentally ill: a literature review,** University of York, Social Policy Research Unit Working Paper 484.

PHILP, M. and DUCKWORTH, D. (1982), *Children with Disabilities and Their Families: A Review of Research*, NFER-Nelson, Windsor.

PUGH, G. with HATTERSLEY, J., TENNANT, L. and WILCOCK, P. (1981), *Parents and Partners: Intervention Schemes and Group Work with Parents of Handicapped Children*, National Childrens Bureau, London.

QUELCH, K. (1981), **A Choice to Stay at Home**, *Health and Social Services Journal*, 29/10/81.

QUINE, L. and PAHL, J. (1985), **Examining the Causes of Stress in Families with Severely Mentally Handicapped Children**, *British Journal of Social Work*, 15: 501-517.

QURESHI, H. and SIMONS, K. (1987), **Resources within families: caring for elderly people**, in Brannen, J. and Wilson, G. (eds), *Give and Take in Families: Studies in Resource Distribution*, Allen and Unwin, London.

QURESHI, H. and WALKER, A. (1989), *The Caring Relationship: Elderly People and Their Families*, Macmillan, London.

RIMMER, L. and WICKS, M. (1983), **The challenge of change: demographic trends, the family and social policy**, in Glennerster, H. (ed), *The Future of the Welfare State: Remaking Social Policy*, Heinemann Educational Books.

ROBINSON, T. and LUSZCZAK, P. (1986), **The Rushcliffe Blend**, *Community Care*, 8/5/86: 18-19.

ROSENBAUM, M. and NAJENSON, T. (1976), **Changes in Life Patterns and Symptoms of Low Mood as Reported by Wives of Severely Brain-Injured Soldiers**, *Journal of Consulting and Clinical Psychology*, 44, 6: 881-8.

RUTTER, M. (1972), *Maternal Deprivation Reassessed*, Penguin Books, Harmondsworth.

RUTTER, M., GRAHAM, P. and YULE, W. (1970), *A Neurophyschiatric Study in Childhood*, Clinics in Developmental Medicine 35/36, London: Spastics International Medical Publishers and Heinemann Medical.

SADDINGTON, N. **Courses for Carers**, *Nursing Times* (Community Outlook), 12/12/84: 434.

SAINSBURY, Sally (1970), **Registered as Disabled**, Occasional Papers on Social Administration No.35, London.

SANDFORD, J.R.A. (1975), **Tolerance of Disability in Elderly Dependants by Supporters at Home: Its Significance for Hospital Practice**, *British Medical Journal*, 3: 471-473.

SCHOFIELD, M. and PRICE, L. (1981a), **Helping Hands at Home**, *Health and Social Services Journal*, 26/6/81: 765-769.

SCHOFIELD, M. and PRICE, L. (1981b), **Nursing Care at Home**, *Health and Social Services Journal*, 17/7/81: 861.

SHANAS, E. (1979), **Social Myth as Hypothesis: The Case of the Family Relations of Old People**, *Gerontologist,* 19: 3-9.

SHELDON, J.H. (1948), *The Social Medicine of Old Age*, The Nuffield Foundation/OUP.

SMITH, G. and CANTLEY, C. (with Ritman, V.) (1983a), *Pluralistic Evaluation: A Study in Day Care for the Elderly Mentally Infirm*, no publisher given.

SMITH, G. and CANTLEY, C. (1983b), **Day Care Made Simple**, *Health and Social Services Journal*, 9/6/83.

SMITH, M. (1983), **Finding the Strength**, *Social Work Today*, 12/7/83.

SMYTH, M. and ROBUS, N. (1989), *The Financial Circumstances of Families with Disabled Children Living in Private Households*, HMSO, London.

TEW, B. and LAURENCE, K.M. (1975), **Some Sources of Stress Found in Mothers of Spina Bifida Children**, *British Journal of Preventative and Social Medicine*, 29: 27-36.

THOMPSON, D.M. and HARAN, D. (1985), **Living With an Amputation: The Helper**, *Social Science and Medicine*, 20, 4: 319-323.

THOMSEN, I.V. (1974), **The Patient with Severe Head Injury and His Family: A Follow-up Study of 50 Patients**, *Scandinavian Journal of Rehabilitation Medicine*, 6: 180-183.

THORNTON, P. (1989) *Creating a Break: A Home Care Relief Scheme for Elderly People and Their Supporters*, Age Concern England, Mitcham.

THORNTON, P. and MOORE, J. (1980), *The Placement of Elderly People in Private Households: An Analysis of Current Provision*, Department of Social Policy & Administration Research Monograph, University of Leeds.

TIDBALL, M. (1981), **For Those on the Borderline**, *Health and Social Services Journal*, 4/9/81: 1077-1079.

TITMUSS, R. (1968), *Commitment to Welfare*, George Allen & Unwin, London.

TOWNSEND, J., HENG, L., THOMAS, T., EGAN, M. and MEADE, T.W. (1981), **Costs of Incontinence to Families with Severely Handicapped Children**, *Community Medicine*, 3: 119-122.

TOWNSEND, P. (1957), *The Family Life of Old People*, Routledge and Kegan Paul, London.

TOWNSEND, P. (1962), *The Last Refuge*, Routledge & Kegan Paul, London.

TOWNSEND, P. (1979), *Poverty in the United Kingdom*, Penguin Books, Harmondsworth.

TOWNSEND, P. (1981), **Elderly people with disabilities**, in Walker, A. and Townsend, P. (eds), *Disability in Britain: A Manifesto of Rights*, Martin Robertson, Oxford.

TWIGG, J. (1988a), **Evaluating Support to Informal Carers: Some Conceptual Issues,** University of York, Social Policy Research Unit, Working Paper DHSS 349.

TWIGG, J. (1989a), **Models of Carers: How do Social Care Agencies Conceptualise their Relationship with Informal Carers**, *Journal of Social Policy*, 18, 1: 53-66.

TWIGG, J. (1989b), **The Evaluation of Support for Informal Carers: Research Review,** University of York, Social Policy Research Unit, Working Paper DHSS 378.

TWIGG, J. (1989c), **Evaluating Services in Support of Informal Carers** in *SPRU and Informal Care*, Social Policy Research Unit, University of York.

TYNE, A. (1982), **Community Care and Mentally Handicapped People**, in Walker, A. (ed), *Community Care: The Family, the State and Social Policy*, Basil Blackwell and Martin Robertson, Oxford.

UNGERSON, C. (1983), **Women and Caring: Skills, Tasks and Taboos** in Gamarnikow, E., Morgan, D., Purvis, J. and Taylorson, D. (eds), *The Public and the Private*, Heinemann, London.

UNGERSON, C. (1987), *Policy is Personal: Sex, Gender and Informal Care*, Tavistock, London.

WADE, D.T., LEGH-SMITH, J. and HEWER, R.L. (1986) **Effects of living with and looking after survivors of a stroke,** *British Medical Journal,* 293: 418-420.

WALKER, Alan (1981), **Community Care and the Elderly in Great Britain: Theory and Practice**, *International Journal of Health Services*, 11, 4: 541- 557.

WALKER, A. (1982), **The Meaning and Social Division of Community Care** in Walker, A. (ed), Community Care: *The Family, the State and Social Policy*, Basil Blackwell and Martin Robertson, Oxford.

WALKER, A. (1983), **Disability and Dependency: A Challenge for the Social Services**, *Research, Policy and Planning*, 1, 1: 1-7.

WARD, L. (1982), *People First: Developing Services in the Community for People with Mental Handicap*, Kings Fund Project Paper No.37, London.

WEEKS, David J. (undated), **Ageism and Being Alone — A Suitable Case for Prevention? (Preliminary Report)**, Jardine Clinic, University of Edinburgh.

WENGER, C. (1984), *The Supportive Network: Coping with Old Age*, George Allen & Unwin, London.

WERTHEIMER, A. (1981), **People with Mental Handicaps** in Walker, A. and Townsend, P. (eds), *Disability in Britain: A Manifesto of Rights*, Martin Robertson, Oxford.

WEST, P. (1984), **The Family, the Welfare State and Community Care: Political Rhetoric & Public Attitudes**, *Journal of Social Policy*, 13, 4: 417- 446.

WEST, P., DALLEY, G., THOMPSON, C., BROWN, S., HEWITT, A., ILLSLEY, R. and KELMAN, H. (1983), **Social Responsibility for the Care of Dependency Groups**, *International Journal of Rehabilitation Research*, 6, 4: 506-7.

WEST, P., ILLSLEY, R. and KELMAN, H. (1984), **Public Preferences for the Care of Dependency Groups**, *Social Science and Medicine*, 18, 4: 287-95.

WICKS, M. (1982), **Community Care and Elderly People** in Walker, A. (ed), *Community Care: The Family, the State and Social Policy*, Basil Blackwell and Martin Robertson, Oxford.

WILKIN, D. (1979), *Caring for the Mentally Handicapped Child*, Croom Helm, London.

WILLMOTT, P. (1986) *Social Networks, Informal Care, and Public Policy*, Policy Studies Institute, London.

WRIGHT, F. (1983), **Single Carers: Employment, Housework and Caring** in Finch, J. and Groves, D. (eds), *A Labour of Love: Women, Work and Caring*, Routledge & Kegan Paul, London.

WRIGHT, K.G., CAIRNS, J.A. and SNELL, M.C. (1981), *Costing Care*, University of Sheffield, Joint Unit for Social Services Research, Social Services Monographs: Research in Practice.

Official Publications

Cmnd 169 *Report of the Royal Commission on Mental Illness & Mental Deficiency*, HMSO, 1957.

Cmnd 1604 *A Hospital Plan for England & Wales*, HMSO 1962.

Cmnd 1973 *Health & Welfare: The Development of Community Care*, HMSO, 1963.

Cmnd 3022 *Health & Welfare: The Development of Community Care, revision to 1975-76 of Plans for the Health & Welfare Services of the Social Authorities in England & Wales*, HMSO, 1966.

Cmnd 3703 *Report of the Committee on Local Authority and Allied Personal Social Services*, HMSO, 1968.

Cmnd 4683 *Better Services for the Mentally Handicapped*, HMSO, 1971.

Cmnd 6233 *Better Services for the Mentally Ill*, HMSO 1975.

Cmnd 8173 *Growing Older*, HMSO, 1981.

DHSS (1976) *Priorities for Health and Personal Social Services in England, A Consultative Document*, HMSO, London.

DHSS (1977) *Priorities in Health and Social Services: The Way Forward*, HMSO, London.

DHSS HM(72)71 *Services for Mental Illness Related to Old Age*, HMSO, London.

DHSS / Welsh Office (1978) *A Happier Old Age, A Discussion Document on Elderly People in our Society*, HMSO, London.

DHSS (1978) *Collaboration in Community Care — A Discussion Document*, HMSO, London.

DHSS (1980), *Mental Handicap: Progress, Problems & Priorities*, HMSO, London.

DHSS (1981), *Care in Action, A Handbook of Policies and Priorities for the Health and Personal Social Services in England*, HMSO, London.

DHSS (1981) *Care in the Community: A Consultative Document on Moving Resources for Care in England*, HMSO, London.

DHSS (1981), *Report of a Study on Community Care*, DHSS, London.

DHSS (1983), Health Circular HC(83)6/LAC(83)5, *Health Service Development, Care in the Community and Joint Finance.*

DEPARTMENT OF HEALTH (1988), *Health and Personal Social Services Statistics for England*, 1988 edition, HMSO, London.

HOUSE OF COMMONS SOCIAL SERVICES COMMITTEE, Second Report 1984-5, *Community care with special reference to adult mentally ill and mentally handicapped people*, vol.1, HMSO, London.

Selected Bibliography

ABRAMS, Philip (1977), **Community Care: Some Research Problems and Priorities**, *Policy and Politics*, 6, 2: 125-151.

ABRAM, P. (ed), BULMER, M. (1984), **Realities of Neighbourhood Care: The Interactions Between Statutory, Voluntary and Informal Social Care**, *Policy and Politics*, 12, 4: 413-429.

ALLAN, G. **Informal Networks of Care: Issues Raised by Barclay**, *British Journal of Social Work*, 13: 417-433.

BARNES, J. and CONNELLY, N. (1978), *Social Care Research: papers and report of a seminar sponsored by the Department of Health and Social Security and organised by the Centre for Studies in Social Policy,* Bedford Square Press, London.

BRIGGS, A. (1983), *Who Cares: Report of a Door-to-Door Survey of People Caring for Dependant Relatives*, Association of Carers, Chatham.

BRIGGS, A. and OLIVER, J. (1985), *Caring: Experiences of Looking After Disabled Relatives*, Routledge & Kegan Paul, London.

BULMER, M. (1987), *The Social Basis of Community Care,* Unwin Hyman, London.

CARTER, J. (1981) *Day Services for Adults: Somewhere to Go*, National Institute Social Services Library No.40, George Allen & Unwin, London.

CECIL, R., OFFER, J. and St. LEGER, F. (1987), *Informal Welfare: A Sociological Study of Care in Northern Ireland*, Gower, Aldershot.

CHEESEMAN, D, LANSLEY J. and WILSON, J. (1972), *Neighbourhood Care and Old People*, Bedford Square Press/ NCSS, London.

GOLDBERG, E.M. and CONNELLY, N. (1981) *Evaluative Research in Social Care*, Heinemann Educational, London.

HENWOOD, M. and WICKS, M. (1984), *The Forgotten Army: Family Care and Elderly People*, Family Policy Studies Centre, London.

HICKS, C. (1988), *Who Cares: Looking After People at Home*, Virago, London.

PARKER, R. (1981), **Tending and Social Policy** in *A New Look at the Personal Social Services,* Goldberg, E.M. and Hatch, S. (eds), *Policy Studies Institute Discussion Paper No.4*, London.

PITKEATHLY, J. (1989) *It's my duty, isn't it? The plight of carers in our society*, Souvenir Press, Oxford.

ROSSITER, C. and WICKS, M. (1982), *Crisis or Challenge? Family Care, Elderly People and Social Policy*, Study Commission on the Family, London.

SEED, P. (1980), *Mental Handicap: Who Helps in Rural and Remote Communities*, Costello Educational, Tunbridge Wells.

THOMPSON, D.M. (1987), *Calling all Carers*, Survey, South Manchester 1985- 6, Report (no publisher given).

TINKER, A. (1984), *Staying at Home: Helping Elderly People*, DOE/HMSO, London.

Some other FPSC publications

Community Care and Elderly People: Policy, Practice and Research Review
Melanie Henwood 1990 £5.45
The publication of the community care White Paper *Caring for People* raises questions of vital importance about the future need for care, and its supply. This review highlights major developments, initiatives, tensions, contradictions and issues in community care with particular reference to elderly people. It raises questions for researchers, policy makers and practitioners alike.

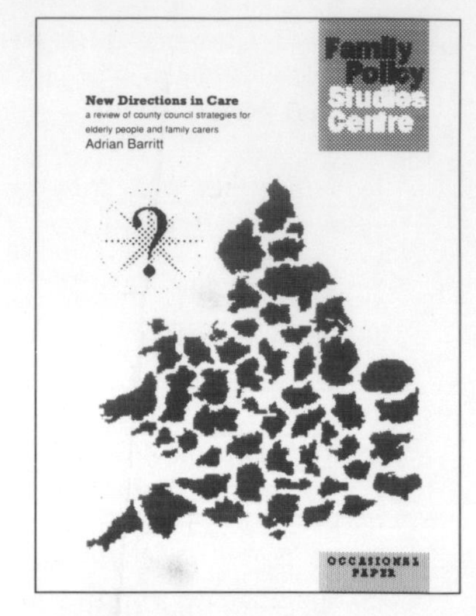

New Directions in Care: A review of county council strategies for elderly people and family carers
Adrian Barritt 1990 £5.00
This review, conducted in 1988/89, provides invaluable information on Counties' plans and policies.
Given the White Paper, *Caring for People*, and new legislation, this report is especially useful and timely.
Many emerging new themes, such as assessment procedures, flexible care packages and joint working are already the focus of much activity on the ground as this review shows.

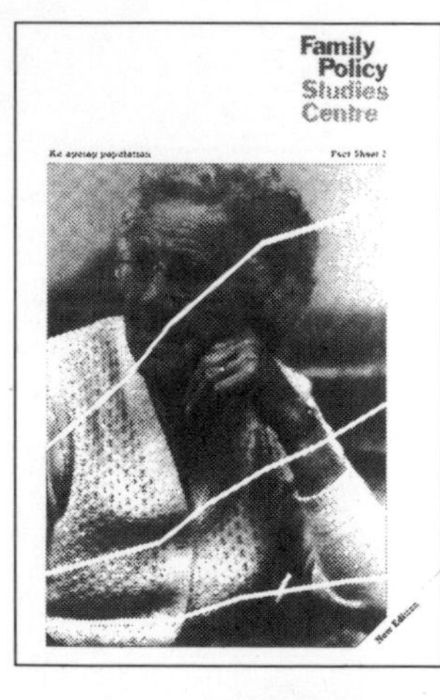

An Ageing Population
1988 £1.00 Fact Sheet
The ageing of the population is a major demographic trend throughout the western world. Increasingly, families today include 3 or 4 generations. The majority of elderly persons continue to live 'In the community', and the support of their families is often vital. This Fact Sheet looks at the size of the elderly population and the characteristics of elderly households, including such topics as housing, income and disability.